**WO**

Printed 1983, 2016

Originally edited by
Vernon Richards
2016 editing and design by
Rob Ray

ISBN 978-1-90-449125-5
All rights reserved

Published by
Freedom Press
84b Whitechapel High St,
London
E1 7QX
freedompress.org.uk

### Editor's notes

The 1983 version of Why Work, edited by Vernon Richards, was a thought-provoking book however some elements of it, including his original introduction, were stacked full of statistics and writing that was laudably up to the minute at the time, but didn't age well. Other pages included letters or illustrations which we can't verify the copyright on. This new version aims to treat Richards' collection sympathetically while cutting, updating, explaining and extending where needed.

Some of the older writers refer to "man" when discussing the whole of humanity, as was customary at the time. We have left this for verisimilitude, but it can be jarring to read today — thank goodness it's no longer the norm.

As was the case in the original, we open with W H Davies ...

~Rob Ray

# LEISURE

*What is this life if, full of care,*
*We have no time to stand and stare.*

*No time to stand beneath the boughs*
*And stare as long as sheep or cows.*

*No time to see, when woods we pass,*
*Where squirrels hide their nuts in grass.*

*No time to see, in broad daylight*
*Streams full of stars, like skies at night.*

*No time to turn at Beauty's glance,*
*And watch her feet, how they can dance.*

*No time to wait till her mouth can*
*Enrich that smile her eyes began.*

*A poor life this if, full of care,*
*We have no time to stand and stare.*

*WH Davies*
*(1870-1940)*

# INTRODUCTION

## BEYOND WAGED LABOUR

*Nina Power*

What do we mean by "work" today? Is there any compelling reason, beyond bare sustenance, why we should do it at all? Most forms of waged labour today are, by all accounts, boring and badly paid. Work is often precarious, with no guarantee that the hours will exist the week after, and with none of the "extras" that secure workers might come to expect — paid holidays, pensions, a guarantee of some form of "security."

Many workers today are on part-time or zero-hours contracts, with little guarantee of even the most minimally-paid work from one day to the next. At the same time, not doing waged labour has become almost impossible (outside of owning a large sum of money already of course), with the unemployed being rebranded as perky "jobseekers," Cognitive Behavioural Therapy prescribed by the state for the most recalcitrant, and all for unlivable amounts of money.

"Hard-working families" are touted as the moral ideal by Conservative and Labour governments alike, and, despite the overwhelming secularism of modern life, work remains a profoundly religious imperative. It is vital that we imagine alternatives to this unhappy situation.

The texts in *Why Work? Arguments for the Leisure Society* may at first glance seem utopian and impractical.

Indeed, whenever anti-work arguments are made, one is met with a familiar set of responses: how will we live if we do not engage in waged labour? Who will do the necessary, unpleasant jobs that humanity cannot do without? If we got rid of work, won't people become lazy and simply descend into idleness and depression? All of these questions are raised and perhaps even answered in the many pieces included here.

In the original Preface to the 1983 edition, Editor Vernon Richards remarked that "[f]or three-quarters of the world's teeming billions, our question [why work?] would be considered a rhetorical one."

In the West, Richards remarks, it is a different story: "A large proportion of existing services and industries in the affluent society could be dispensed without society being any the poorer."

There is a simple test, he suggests — ask yourself what would disrupt your life more? A strike by miners or Fleet Street print workers? A strike by farmers or workers in the arms industry? A strike by dustmen or asset strippers?

## A Faded Promise

Since the book's first publication, however, history has unfortunately demonstrated how uselessness has replaced use, as industry and production has been violently swept aside in favour of precisely those forms of labour that deal not primarily with materials and people but with greed and war.

Lately there has been much discussion of "automation" — the idea that much work can be handed over to the machines without the need for human labour — but this discussion has been around for much longer than we might first imagine. Richards notes that "robotisation" simply "dumps more workers on the scrap heap." Yet today we seem to have a curious combination of automation without the concomitant reduction in labour hours: many people are engaged in what can only be described, as David Graeber puts it in his essay, "bullshit jobs" as follows:

> In the year 1930, John Maynard Keynes predicted that technology would have advanced sufficiently by century's end that countries like Great Britain or the United States would achieve a 15-hour work week. There's every reason to believe he was right. In technological terms, we are quite capable of this.
>
> And yet it didn't happen. Instead, technology has been marshaled, if anything, to figure out ways to make us all work more. In order to achieve this, jobs have had to be created that are, effectively, pointless. Huge swathes of people, in Europe and North America in particular, spend their entire working lives performing tasks they secretly believe do not really need to be performed. The moral and spiritual damage that comes from this situation is profound. It is a scar across our collective soul. Yet virtually no-one talks about it.

Can we liberate technology or should we return to a simpler way of life? It is hard to imagine a world without mobile phones, laptops, washing machines, cars, etc., though of course these things are extremely unevenly distributed on a global scale. Anarcho-primitivism nevertheless offers one way of thinking about a way of living without technology.

One of its leading proponents, John Zerzan, argues that life in prehistory was not "nasty, brutish and short," as philosopher Thomas Hobbes had it, but rather egalitarian and peaceful:

> Since the mid-1960s there has been a paradigm shift in how anthropologists understand prehistory, with profound implications for theory. Based on a solid body of archaeological and ethnographic research, mainstream anthropology has abandoned the Hobbesian hypothesis. Life before or outside civilisation is now defined more specifically as social existence prior to domestication of animals and plants.

Mounting evidence demonstrates that before the Neolithic shift from a foraging or gatherer-hunter mode of existence to an agricultural lifeway, most people had ample free time, considerable gender autonomy or equality, an ethos of egalitarianism and sharing, and no organised violence.

For many Marxists and modernists, however, imagining a prelapsarian time before industry, expropriation, slavery, technology and the alarm clock remains strictly fantastical, though there are of course still a significant amount of people who live "off-grid" or in religious and non-religious communes that aim to be as self-sufficient as possible. Feminism, particularly in its Marxist and anarchist versions, has dramatically improved and expanded the notion of "work" as traditionally conceived. Waged labour — selling labour power in return for a wage — is, as many feminists have pointed out, only a small proportion of the work that is done on a daily basis. The billions of hours of unpaid labour that go into reproducing life as such, everything from childbirth to emotional labour, cleaning and cooking to caring, work that historically has been gendered female, and racialised in certain ways, what gets called "social reproduction." As Ferguson and McNally put it:

> [T]he social reproduction approach transforms our understanding of labour-power. In conventional Marxist analyses, labour-power is simply presumed to be present — a given factor of capitalist production.
>
> At best, it is understood as the product of natural, biologically determined, regenerative processes. In socialising labour-power — in unearthing its insertion in history, society, and culture — social reproduction feminism reveals, in the first instance, that labour-power cannot simply be presumed to exist, but is made available to capital only because of its reproduction in and through a particular set of gendered and sexualised social relations that exist beyond the direct labour/capital relation, in the so-called private sphere. It also sharpens our understanding of the contradictory position of labour-power with respect to capital — identifying all aspects of our social reproduction — of our quest to satisfy human needs, to live — as essential to, but also a drag on, accumulation (because capital pays indirectly for this through wages, benefits, and taxes).

As well as expanding the concept of work to include unwaged labour, social reproduction feminism also complicates workplace struggles. We might imagine the laying down of tools at a factory or the sabotage of machines, but it is a different thing altogether to imagine what it might mean to go on a "care strike," if what that would mean is the abandonment of vulnerable people to their fates: babies, children, the elderly and the sick. Nor can technology fully automate the forms of labour that make up social reproduction.

As Federici puts it with reference to elderly care: "Only in part can the needs and desires of non-self-sufficient older people, or people requiring medical assistance, be addressed by incorporating technologies into the work by which they are reproduced."

## FALC and the Universal Basic Income

Nevertheless, despite this important feminist work, we are currently surrounded by calls for "full automation" as part of a project of "Fully Automated Luxury Communism" (FALC). As Aaron Bastani put it: 'the only utopian demand can be for the full automation of everything and common ownership of that which is automated."

As deliriously exciting as FALC sounds, full automation remains something of a techno-fantasy, ignoring the real needs of human beings. While it may be perfectly possible to have robots look after babies and older people, would it be desirable? What about the delights of freely-chosen human interaction? Of friendship? Of love and care and playfulness?

Alongside the allure of full automation as a solution to tiresome labour is the rather more practical, if indeed still somewhat improbable, suggestion of Universal Basic Income (UBI). Here every citizen of a particular country would be guaranteed a stipend, an amount that would render life liveable at a minimal level. The immediate sting of unemployment would be removed and poverty would be eliminated, ideally.

Those who chose to work could do so on top of the basic income. UBI has been proposed by both left and right-wing governments as both egalitarian and libertarian. The recent re-emergence of interest in the idea may have come about partly because of fears of automation. As Bhaskar Sunkara puts it: "People are fearful of becoming redundant, and there's this sense that the economy can't be built to provide jobs for everyone" and a UBI project may even help to build "social solidarity" as the worst excesses of poverty are ameliorated.

While UBI appears to offer a practical solution to the call to work less, some have recently criticised it as a cover-story for further neoliberal reforms. As Dmytri Kleiner puts it: "[T]he reason many people on the left are excited about proposals such as universal basic income is that they acknowledge economic inequality and its social consequences. However, a closer look at how UBI is expected to work reveals that it is intended to provide political cover for the elimination of social programs and the privatization of social services."

UBI could also simply raise prices, particularly of necessities such as housing. The poor would ultimately still be worse off and welfare provision could be eliminated for specific and costly needs such as those relating to disability.

Where UBI has been proposed, such as in Switzerland recently, right-wing opponents of the scheme argued that it would prove too attractive to migrants. It is evident that a neoliberal and right-wing programme could use UBI as a way of arguing for a closing of the borders, awarding it only to "citizens" of a particular country. More radical in this regard is the proposal for a Global Basic Income (GBI) which would guarantee an unconditional basic minimum income to people in all countries. The Global Basic Income Foundation proposes initially that this would be around $1 a day — clearly this would not have much impact on people living in the richer Global North, but the Foundation argue that it would end the extreme poverty of the 1 billion people who currently live on less than $1 a day.

More radical still would be the re-appropriation of all land, time and resources that have been stolen from the people by colonialism, capitalism and slavery. It is clear that there is more than enough to go around if materials and property were reclaimed by the people. It is both easy and difficult to imagine a world without the need to sell one's labour power (and a world without money), where gruelling, pointless and endless waged labour was replaced by something altogether more enjoyable — human activity as such, the exploration of our powers and capacities in various directions. Waged work ties us to particular repetitive activities and roles, but in a world in which human activity was directed at the direct sustaining of life and not to the generation of profit, we could explore our abilities to both be together and to develop our individual potentials.

### The Selected Works

*Why Work?* brings together various different critical approaches to the question of work. Some might seem more utopian or distant than others, but all have at their heart the idea that life can and must be lived differently, and that there is no inherent moral value to waged labour, and indeed, this kind of work often generates real harm.

Bertrand Russell in his famous essay *In Praise of Idleness* (1932) suggests that "[t]he morality of work is the morality of slaves, and the modern world has no need of slavery." While we might want to draw a sharp distinction between historical slavery and the metaphorical sense used by Russell here, it is clear that the world of "idleness" or leisure that Russell imagines in a world without waged labour, or where only a small portion of the day is taken up in necessary labour, will be a world in which there will be "happiness and joy of life, instead of frayed nerves, weariness and dyspepsia. The work exacted will be enough to make leisure delightful, but not enough to produce exhaustion ... Ordinary men and women, having the opportunity of a happy life, will become more kindly and less persecuting and less inclined to view others with suspicion."

William Morris too, in his lecture from 1885, *Useless Work Versus Useless Toil*, praises what he calls the "ornamental" part of life — the work that we willingly take on because it is pleasurable. Again, strictly necessary work would, in Morris's image, take up only a small part of each day, and the rest could be given over to pleasures of all kinds.

Other texts tackle the reality and history of work. George Woodcock in *The Tyranny of the Clock* (1944) points out that the invention of a particular conception of time and measurement has actually generated a form of repetitive work in which "[m]en actually became like clocks." Quantity has replaced quality — liberation from mechanical time would involve not only freeing humanity from rulers and managers but also from abstractions such as time itself.

Berneri's essay The Problem of Work proposes an alternative to repetitious labour, whose deleterious psychological and physical effects he outlines. This he calls "attractive work," taking as his model the work already performed by "the scientists, the thinkers, and the artists." Berneri defends work freely chosen and performed without compulsion, and presents the formula "no compulsion to work, but no duty towards those who do not want to work."

Ifan Edwards's The Art of Shovelling presents a descriptive account of his time as a manual labourer, while John Hewetson in Measuring Misery (1954) attempts to analyse the sheer amount of misery generated by the status quo. Kropotkin's The Wage System (1888) surveys various political responses to the question of the wage, calling for "communism and anarchy" not "individualism and authority."

Posing one of the trickier questions, Tony Gibson in Who Will Do the Dirty Work? (1952), suggests that part of the problem lies in the social attitude we have towards supposedly undesirable jobs. Agreeing with the idea, already encountered in Morris, Beneri and others, that freedom must involve the absence of coercion to work, Gibson proposes that "the only justification for work is that we enjoy it," and that work itself must become a kind of play and enjoyment, even that work which we now resent.

In Alternatives and Futures, we are presented with various positive images and experiments in anti-waged labour. In Reflections on Utopia (1962), SF examines the Kibbutzim in Israel, arguing that the collective way of life exhibited there shows that "people are in fact capable of living a new way of life" without money, private property or written laws. Gaston Leval's piece on Collectives in the Spanish Revolution (1975) similarly examines the role of the collective in Aragon and elsewhere, stressing their relation to "universal solidarity" in the form of a recognition that liberty only exists "as a function of practical activity," and not as a negative liberty.

Elsewhere, there is discussion of the "self-build" movement, of leisure as a positive concept stretching all the way back to the Greeks, of the "other economy" of unemployment and its relation to wealth-generation beyond waged labour, and finally, we have a collection of editorials from Freedom Newspaper (1958-62) entitled Production: Use vs Profit, where the idea of full employment is criticised and demands are made instead for access to the necessities of life as a right.

As the final piece concludes: "Anarchism is not the struggle for better wages, more gadgets and full employment. It is the struggle to win the freedom to dispose of one's own time. Time is not money; time is Life."

In this updated edition of the collection, new pieces appear which go some way to rendering the pieces more up to date as well as partly correcting the gender bias of the original collection. Here we have an extract from famed sociologist Juliet Schor's 1990s writings on overwork, Claire Wolfe's *Dark Satanic Cubicles* (2005) which suggests that we need to smash the "job culture" that sees us shackled to our desks and chained to misery, and Voltarine De Cleyre's thinking on the difference in vision between modern toil and the works of ages past. Sprinkled throughout are various anti-work drawings and diagrams.

The discussion about what work means, and how we can avoid its painful, boring and oppressive aspects is one that has a long history, and ever-pressing future. *Why Work?* asks difficult questions and offers bright and optimistic answers. Long may everyone enjoy as much of their time as they can, in work and at play!

# IN PRAISE OF IDLENESS

*Bertrand Russell*

*Bertrand Russell (1872-1970) was one of the most famous British philosophers and mathematicians of the twentieth century. This well-known essay was first published by Harper's Magazine (US) in 1932. We have omitted what the author himself referred to as "only preliminary" (about 10%) but included all that "I want to say, in all seriousness" (90%).*

A great deal of harm is being done in the modern world by belief in the virtuousness of WORK, and that the road to happiness and prosperity lies in an organised diminution of work.

First of all: what is work?

Work is of two kinds: first, altering the position of matter at or near the earth's surface relatively to other such matter; second, telling other people to do so. The first kind is unpleasant and ill paid, the second is pleasant and highly paid. The second kind is capable of indefinite extension: there are not only those who give orders, but those who give advice as to what orders should be given. Usually two opposite kinds of advice are given simultaneously by two organised bodies of men; this is called politics. The skill required for this kind of work is not knowledge of the subjects as to which advice is given, but knowledge of the art of persuasive speaking and writing, i.e. of advertising.

Throughout Europe, though not in America, there is a third class of men, more respected than either of the classes of workers. There are men who, through ownership of land, are able to make others pay for the privilege of being allowed to exist and to work. These landowners are idle, and I might therefore be expected to praise them. Unfortunately, their idleness is only rendered possible by the industry of others; indeed their desire for comfortable idleness is historically the source of the whole gospel of work. The last thing they have ever wished is that others should follow their example.

From the beginning of civilisation until the Industrial Revolution, a man could, as a rule, produce by hard work little more than was required for the subsistence of himself and his family, although his wife worked at least as hard as he did, and his children added their labour as soon as they were old enough to do so.

The small surplus above bare necessaries was not left to those who produced it, but was appropriated by warriors and priests. In times of famine there was no surplus; the warriors and priests, however, still secured as much as at other times, with the result that many of the workers died of hunger. This system persisted in Russia until 1917,[1] and still persists in the East; in England, in spite of the Industrial Revolution, it remained in full force throughout the Napoleonic wars, and until a hundred years ago, when the new class of manufacturers acquired power.

In America, the system came to an end with the revolution, except in the South, where it persisted until the Civil War. A system which lasted so long and ended so recently has naturally left a profound impress upon men's thoughts and opinions. Much that we take for granted about the desirability of work is derived from this system, and, being pre-industrial, is not adapted to the modern world. Modern technique has made it possible for leisure, within limits, to be not the prerogative of small privileged classes, but a right evenly distributed throughout the community. The morality of work is the morality of slaves, and the modern world has no need of slavery.

It is obvious that, in primitive communities, peasants, left to themselves, would not have parted with the slender surplus upon which the warriors and priests subsisted, but would have either produced less or consumed more. At first, sheer force compelled them to produce and part with the surplus. Gradually, however, it was found possible to induce many of them to accept an ethic according to which it was their duty to work hard, although part of their work went to support others in idleness. By this means the amount of compulsion required was lessened, and the expenses of government were diminished.

To this day, 99% of British wage-earners would be genuinely shocked if it were proposed that the King should not have larger income than a working man. The conception of duty, speaking historically, has been a means used by the holders of power to induce others to live for the interests of their masters rather than for their own. Of course the holders of power conceal this fact from themselves by managing to believe that their interests are identical with the larger interests of humanity.

Sometimes this is true; Athenian slave-owners, for instance, employed part of their leisure in making a permanent contribution to civilisation which would have been impossible under a just economic system. Leisure is essential to civilisation, and in former times leisure for the few was only rendered possible by the labours of the many. But their labours were valuable, not because work is good, but because leisure is good. And with modern technique it would be possible to distribute leisure justly without injury to civilisation.

Modern technique has made it possible to diminish enormously the amount of labour required to secure the necessaries of life for everyone. This was made obvious during the war. At that time, all the men in the armed forces, all the men and women engaged in the production of munitions, all the men and women engaged in spying, war propaganda, or Government offices connected with the war, were withdrawn from productive occupation.

In spite of this, the general level of physical well-being among unskilled wage-earners on the side of the Allies was higher than before or since. The significance of this fact was concealed by finance: borrowing made it appear as if the future was nourishing the present. But that, of course, would have been impossible; a man cannot eat a loaf of bread that does not yet exist.

The war showed conclusively that, by the scientific organisation of production, it is possible to keep modern populations in fair comfort on a small part of the working capacity of the modern world. If, at the end of the war, the scientific organisation, which had been created in order to liberate men for fighting and munition work, had been preserved, and the hours of work had been cut down to four, all would have been well. Instead of that the old chaos was restored, those whose work was demanded were made to work long hours, and the rest were left to starve as unemployed. Why? Because work is a duty, and a man should not receive wages in proportion to what he has produced, but in proportion to his virtue as exemplified by his industry.

This is the morality of the Slave State, applied in circumstances totally unlike those in which it arose. No wonder the result has been disastrous. Let us take an illustration. Suppose that, at a given moment, a certain number of people are engaged in the manufacture of pins. They make as many pins as the world needs, working (say) eight hours a day. Someone makes an invention by which the same number of men can make twice as many pins as before. But the world does not need twice as many pins: pins are already so cheap that hardly any more will be bought at a lower price. In a sensible world, everybody concerned in the manufacture of pins would take to working four hours instead of eight, and everything else would go on as before. But in the actual world this would be thought demoralizing. The men still work eight hours, there are too many pins, some employers go bankrupt, and half the men previously concerned in making pins are thrown out of work. There is, in the end, just as much leisure as on the other plan, but half the men are totally idle while half are still overworked. In this way, it is insured that the unavoidable leisure shall cause misery all round instead of being a universal source of happiness. Can anything more insane be imagined?

The idea that the poor should have leisure has always been shocking to the rich. In England, in the early nineteenth century, fifteen hours was the ordinary day's work for a man; children sometimes did as much, and very commonly did twelve hours a day. When meddlesome busybodies suggested that perhaps these hours were rather long, they were told that work kept adults from drink and children from mischief. When I was a child, shortly after urban working men had acquired the vote, certain public holidays were established by law, to the great indignation of the upper classes. I remember hearing an old Duchess say: "What do the poor want with holidays? They ought to work." People nowadays are less frank, but the sentiment persists, and is the source of much of our economic confusion.

Let us, for a moment, consider the ethics of work frankly, without superstition. Every human being, of necessity, consumes, in the course of his life, a certain amount of the produce of human labour. Assuming, as we may, that labour is on the whole disagreeable, it is unjust that a man should consume more than he produces. Of course he may provide services rather than commodities, like a medical man, for example; but he should provide something in return for his board and lodging.

To this extent, the duty of work must be admitted, but to this extent only.

I shall not dwell upon the fact that, in all modern societies outside the USSR, many people escape even this minimum of work, namely all those who inherit money and all those who marry money. I do not think the fact that these people are allowed to be idle is nearly so harmful as the fact that wage-earners are expected to overwork or starve.

If the ordinary wage-earner worked four hours a day, there would be enough for everybody, and no unemployment — assuming a certain very moderate amount of sensible organisation. This idea shocks the well-to-do, because they are convinced that the poor would not know how to use so much leisure. In America, men often work long hours even when they are already well off; such men, naturally, are indignant at the idea of leisure for wage-earners, except as the grim punishment of unemployment; in fact, they dislike leisure even for their sons.

Oddly enough, while they wish their sons to work so hard as to have no time to be civilised, they do not mind their wives and daughters having no work at all. The snobbish admiration of uselessness, which, in an aristocratic society, extends to both sexes, is, under a plutocracy, confined to women; this, however, does not make it any more in agreement with common sense.

The wise use of leisure, it must be conceded, is a product of civilisation and education. A man who has worked long hours all his life will be bored if he becomes suddenly idle. But without a considerable amount of leisure a man is cut off from many of the best things. There is no longer any reason why the bulk of the population should suffer this deprivation; only a foolish asceticism, usually vicarious, makes us continue to insist on work in excessive quantities now that the need no longer exists.

In the new creed which controls the government of Russia, while there is much that is very different from the traditional teaching of the West, there are some things that are quite unchanged.

The attitude of the governing classes, and especially of those who conduct educational propaganda, on the subject of the dignity of labour, is almost exactly that which the governing classes of the world have always preached to what were called the "honest poor." Industry, sobriety, willingness to work long hours for distant advantages, even submissiveness to authority, all these reappear; moreover authority still represents the will of the Ruler of the Universe, Who, however, is now called by a new name, Dialectical Materialism.

The victory of the proletariat in Russia has some points in common with the victory of the feminists in some other countries. For ages, men had conceded the superior saintliness of women, and had consoled women for their inferiority by maintaining that saintliness is more desirable than power. At last the feminists decided that they would have both, since the pioneers among them believed all that the men had told them about the desirability of virtue, but not what they had told them about the worthlessness of political power. A similar thing has happened in Russia as regards manual work.

For ages, the rich and their sycophants have written in praise of "honest toil," have praised the simple life, have professed a religion which teaches that the poor are much more likely to go to heaven than the rich, and in general have tried to make manual workers believe that there is some special nobility about altering the position of matter in space, just as men tried to make women believe that they derived some special nobility from their sexual enslavement. In Russia, all this teaching about the excellence of manual work has been taken seriously, with the result that the manual worker is more honoured than anyone else. What are, in essence, revivalist appeals are made, but not for the old purposes: they are made to secure shock workers for special tasks. Manual work is the ideal which is held before the young, and is the basis of all ethical teaching.

For the present, possibly, this is all to the good. A large country, full of natural resources, awaits development, and has to be developed with very little use of credit. In these circumstances, hard work is necessary, and is likely to bring a great reward. But what will happen when the point has been reached where everybody could be comfortable without working long hours?

In the West, we have various ways of dealing with this problem. We have no attempt at economic justice, so that a large proportion of the total produce goes to a small minority of the population, many of whom do no work at all. Owing to the absence of any central control over production, we produce hosts of things that are not wanted. We keep a large percentage of the working population idle, because we can dispense with their labour by making the others overwork. When all these methods prove inadequate, we have a war: we cause a number of people to manufacture high explosives, and a number of others to explode them, as if we were children who had just discovered fireworks. By a combination of all these devices we manage, though with difficulty, to keep alive the notion that a great deal of severe manual work must be the lot of the average man.

In Russia, owing to more economic justice and central control over production, the problem will have to be differently solved. The rational solution would be, as soon as the necessaries and elementary comforts can be provided for all, to reduce the hours of labour gradually, allowing a popular vote to decide, at each stage, whether more leisure or more goods were to be preferred. But, having taught the supreme virtue of hard work, it is difficult to see how the authorities can aim at a paradise in which there will be much leisure and little work. It seems more likely that they will find continually fresh schemes, by which present leisure is to be sacrificed to future productivity.

I read recently of an ingenious plan put forward by Russian engineers, for making the White Sea and the northern coasts of Siberia warm, by putting a dam across the Kara Sea. An admirable project, but liable to postpone proletarian comfort for a generation, while the nobility of toil is being displayed amid the ice-fields and snowstorms of the Arctic Ocean. This sort of thing, if it happens, will be the result of regarding the virtue of hard work as an end in itself, rather than as a means to a state of affairs in which it is no longer needed.

The fact is that moving matter about, while a certain amount of it is necessary to our existence, is emphatically not one of the ends of human life. If it were, we should have to consider every navvy superior to Shakespeare. We have been misled in this matter by two causes. One is the necessity of keeping the poor contented, which has led the rich, for thousands of years, to preach the dignity of labour, while taking care themselves to remain undignified in this respect.

The other is the new pleasure in mechanism, which makes us delight in the astonishingly clever changes that we can produce on the earth's surface. Neither of these motives makes any great appeal to the actual workers. If you ask him what he thinks the best part of his life, he is not likely to say: "I enjoy manual work because it makes me feel that I am fulfilling man's noblest task, and because I like to think how much man can transform his planet. It is true that my body demands periods of rest, which I have to fill in as best I may, but I am never so happy as when the morning comes and I can return to the toil from which my contentment springs." I have never heard working men say this sort of thing. They consider work, as it should be considered, a necessary means to a livelihood, and it is from their leisure hours that they derive whatever happiness they may enjoy.

It will be said that, while a little leisure is pleasant, men would not know how to fill their days if they had only four hours of work out of the twenty-four. In so far as this is true in the modern world, it is a condemnation of our civilisation; it would not have been true at any earlier period. There was formerly a capacity for light-heartedness and play which has been to some extent inhibited by the cult of efficiency.

The modern man thinks that everything ought to be done for the sake of something else, and never for its own sake. Serious-minded persons, for example, are continually condemning the habit of going to the cinema, and telling us that it leads the young into crime. But all the work that goes to producing a cinema is respectable, because it is work, and because it brings a money profit. The notion that the desirable activities are those that bring a profit has made everything topsy-turvy. The butcher who provides you with meat and the baker who provides you with bread are praiseworthy, because they are making money; but when you enjoy the food they have provided, you are merely frivolous, unless you eat only to get strength for your work. Broadly speaking, it is held that getting money is good and spending money is bad. Seeing that they are two sides of one transaction, this is absurd; one might as well maintain that keys are good, but keyholes are bad.

Whatever merit there may be in the production of goods must be entirely derivative from the advantage to be obtained by consuming them. The individual, in our society, works for profit; but the social purpose of his work lies in the consumption of what he produces. It is this divorce between the individual and the social purpose of production that makes it so difficult for men to think clearly in a world in which profit-making is the incentive to industry. We think too much of production, and too little of consumption.

One result is that we attach too little importance to enjoyment and simple happiness; and that we do not judge production by the pleasure that it gives to the consumer.

When I suggest that working hours should be reduced to four, I am not meaning to imply that all the remaining time should necessarily be spent in pure frivolity. I mean that four hours' work a day should entitle a man to the necessities and elementary comforts of life, and that the rest of his time should be his to use as he might see fit.

It is an essential part of any such social system that education should be carried further than it usually is at present, and should aim, in part, at providing tastes which would enable a man to use leisure intelligently. I am not thinking mainly of the sort of things that would be considered "highbrow." Peasant dances have died out except in remote rural areas, but the impulses which caused them to be cultivated must still exist in human nature. The pleasures of urban populations have become mainly passive: seeing cinemas, watching football matches, listening to the radio, and so on. This results from the fact that their active energies are fully taken up with work; if they had more leisure, they would again enjoy pleasures in which they took an active part. In the past, there was a small leisure class and a larger working class. The leisure class enjoyed advantages for which there was no basis in social justice; this necessarily made it oppressive, limited its sympathies, and caused it to invent theories by which to justify its privileges.

These facts greatly diminished its excellence, but in spite of this drawback it contributed nearly the whole of what we call civilisation. It cultivated the arts and discovered the sciences; it wrote the books, invented the philosophies, and refined social relations. Even the liberation of the oppressed has usually been inaugurated from above. Without the leisure class, mankind would never have emerged from barbarism.

The method of a hereditary leisure class without duties was, however, extraordinarily wasteful. None of the members of the class had been taught to be industrious, and the class as a whole was not exceptionally intelligent. The class might produce one Darwin, but against him had to be set tens of thousands of country gentlemen who never thought of anything more intelligent than fox-hunting and punishing poachers. At present, the universities are supposed to provide, in a more systematic way, what the leisure class provided accidentally and as a by-product.

This is a great improvement, but it has certain drawbacks. University life is so different from life in the world at large that men who live in an academic milieu tend to be unaware of the preoccupations and problems of ordinary men and women; moreover their ways of expressing themselves are usually such as to rob their opinions of the influence that they ought to have upon the general public. Another disadvantage is that in universities studies are organised, and the man who thinks of some original line of research is likely to be discouraged. Academic institutions, therefore, useful as they are, are not adequate guardians of the interests of civilisation in a world where everyone outside their walls is too busy for unutilitarian pursuits.

In a world where no one is compelled to work more than four hours a day, every person possessed of scientific curiosity will be able to indulge it, and every painter will be able to paint without starving, however excellent his pictures may be.

Young writers will not be obliged to draw attention to themselves by sensational pot-boilers, with a view to acquiring the economic independence needed for monumental works, for which, when the time at last comes, they will have lost the taste and the capacity. Men who, in their professional work, have become interested in some phase of economics of government, will be able to develop their ideas without the academic detachment that makes the work of university economists often seem lacking in reality. Medical men will have time to learn about the progress of medicine, teachers will not be exasperatedly struggling to teach by routine methods things which they learnt in their youth, which may, in the interval have been proved to be untrue.

Above all, there will be happiness and joy of life, instead of frayed nerves, weariness, and dyspepsia. The work exacted will be enough to make leisure delightful, but not enough to produce exhaustion. Since men will not be tired in their spare time, they will not demand only such amusements as are passive and vapid. At least 1% will probably devote the time not spent in professional work to pursuits of some public importance, and, since they will not depend upon these pursuits for their livelihood, their originality will be unhampered, and there will be no need to conform to the standards set by elderly pundits.

But it is not only in these exceptional cases that the advantages of leisure will appear. Ordinary men and women, having the opportunity of a happy life, will become more kindly and less persecuting and less inclined to view others with suspicion. The taste for war will die out, partly for this reason, and partly because it will involve long and severe work for all. Good nature is, of all moral qualities, the one that the world needs most, and good nature is the result of ease and security, not of a life of arduous struggle.

Modern methods of production have given us the possibility of ease and security for all; we have chosen, instead, to have overwork for some and starvation for others. Hitherto we have continued to be as energetic as we were before there were machines; in this we have been foolish, but there is no reason to go on being foolish forever.

1. Since then, members of the Communist Party have succeeded to this privilege of the warriors and priests.

# USEFUL WORK VERSUS USELESS TOIL

*William Morris*

*Morris (1834-1896) was one of the founders of the Arts and Crafts Movement, and a major figure in early British socialism. Given as a lecture in 1884, this work was first published as a Commonweal pamphlet in a series with the general title* The Socialist Platform *in 1885.*

The above title may strike some of my readers as strange. It is assumed by most people nowadays that all work is useful, and by most well-to-do people that all work is desirable. Most people, well-to-do or not, believe that, even when a man is doing work which appears to be useless, he is earning his livelihood by it — he is "employed," as the phrase goes; and most of those who are well-to-do cheer on the happy worker with congratulations and praises, if he is only "industrious" enough and deprives himself of all pleasure and holidays in the sacred cause of labour. In short, it has become an article of the creed of modern morality that all labour is good in itself — a convenient belief to those who live on the labour of others. But as to those on whom they live, I recommend them not to take it on trust, but to look into the matter a little deeper.

Let us grant, first, that the race of man must either labour or perish. Nature does not give us our livelihood gratis; we must win it by toil of some sort or degree. Let us see, then, if she does not give us some compensation for this compulsion to labour, since certainly in other matters she takes care to make the acts necessary to the continuance of life in the individual and the race not only endurable, but even pleasurable.

You may be sure that she does so, that it is the nature of man, when he is not diseased, to take pleasure in his work under certain conditions. And, yet, we must say in the teeth of the hypocritical praise of all labour, whatsoever it may be, of which I have made mention, that there is some labour which is so far from being a blessing that it is a curse; that it would be better for the community and for the worker if the latter were to fold his hands and refuse to work, and either die or let us pack him off to the workhouse or prison — which you will.

Here, you see, are two kinds of work — one good, the other bad; one not far removed from a blessing, a lightening of life; the other a mere curse, a burden to life.

What is the difference between them, then? This one has hope in it, the other has not. It is manly to do the one kind of work, and manly also to refuse to do the other. What is the nature of the hope which, when it is present in work, makes it worth doing?

It is threefold, I think — hope of rest, hope of product, hope of pleasure in the work itself; and hope of these also in some abundance and of good quality; rest enough and good enough to be worth having; product worth having by one who is neither a fool nor an ascetic; pleasure enough for all of us to be conscious of it while we are at work; not a mere habit, the loss of which we shall feel as a fidgety man feels the loss of the bit of string he fidgets with.

I have put the hope of rest first because it is the simplest and most natural part of our hope. Whatever pleasure there is in some work, there is certainly some pain in all work, the beast-like pain of stirring up our slumbering energies to action, the beast-like dread of change when things are pretty well with us; and the compensation for this animal pain in animal rest. We must feel while we are working that the time will come when we shall not have to work.

Also the rest, when it comes, must be long enough to allow us to enjoy it; it must be longer than is merely necessary for us to recover the strength we have expended in working, and it must be animal rest also in this, that it must not be disturbed by anxiety, else we shall not be able to enjoy it. If we have this amount and kind of rest we shall, so far, be no worse off than the beasts.

As to the hope of product, I have said that Nature compels us to work for that. It remains for us to look to it that we do really produce something, and not nothing, or at least nothing that we want or are allowed to use. If we look to this and use our wills we shall, so far, be better than machines.

The hope of pleasure in the work itself: how strange that hope must seem to some of my readers — to most of them! Yet I think that to all living things there is a pleasure in the exercise of their energies, and that even beasts rejoice in being lithe and swift and strong. But a man at work, making something which he feels will exist because he is working at it and wills it, is exercising the energies of his mind and soul as well as of his body. Memory and imagination help him as he works. Not only his own thoughts, but the thoughts of the men of past ages guide his hands; and, as a part of the human race, he creates. If we work thus we shall be men, and our days will be happy and eventful.

Thus worthy work carries with it the hope of pleasure in rest, the hope of the pleasure in our using what it makes, and the hope of pleasure in our daily creative skill. All other work but this is worthless; it is slaves' work — mere toiling to live, that we may live to toil.

Therefore, since we have, as it were, a pair of scales in which to weigh the work now done in the world, let us use them. Let us estimate the worthiness of the work we do, after so many thousand years of toil, so many promises of hope deferred, such boundless exultation over the progress of civilisation and the gain of liberty.

Now, the first thing as to the work done in civilisation and the easiest to notice is that it is portioned out very unequally amongst the different classes of society. First, there are people — not a few — who do no work, and make no pretence of doing any. Next, there are people, and very many of them, who work fairly hard, though with abundant easements and holidays, claimed and allowed; and lastly, there are people who work so hard that they may be said to do nothing else than work, and are accordingly called "the working classes," as distinguished from the middle classes and the rich, or aristocracy, whom I have mentioned above.

It is clear that this inequality presses heavily upon the 'working' class, and must visibly tend to destroy their hope of rest at least, and so, in that particular, make them worse off than mere beasts of the field; but that is not the sum and end of our folly of turning useful work into useless toil, but only the beginning of it.

For first, as to the class of rich people doing no work, we all know that they consume a great deal while they produce nothing. Therefore, clearly, they have to be kept at the expense of those who do work, just as paupers have, and are a mere burden on the community. In these days there are many who have learned to see this, though they can see no further into the evils of our present system, and have formed no idea of any scheme for getting rid of this burden; though perhaps they have a vague hope that changes in the system of voting for members of the House of Commons, may, as if by magic, tend in that direction. With such hopes or superstitions we need not trouble ourselves. Moreover, this class, the aristocracy, once thought most necessary to the State of is scant numbers, and has now no power of its own, but depends on the support of the class next below it — the middle class. In fact, it is really composed either of the most successful men of that class, or of their immediate descendants.

As to the middle class, including the trading, manufacturing, and professional people of our society, they do, as a rule, seem to work quite hard enough, and so at first sight might be thought to help the community, and not burden it. But by far the greater part of them, though they work, do not produce, and even when they do produce, as in the case of those engaged (wastefully indeed) in the distribution of goods, or doctors, or (genuine) artists and literary men, they consume out of all proportion to their due share.

The commercial and manufacturing part of them, the most powerful part, spend their lives and energies in fighting among themselves for their respective shares of the wealth which they force the genuine workers to provide for them; the others are almost wholly the hangers-on of these; they do not work for the public, but a privileged class: they are the parasites of property, sometimes, as in the case of lawyers, undisguisedly so; sometimes, as the doctors and others above mentioned, professing to be useful, but too often of no use save as supporters of the system of folly, fraud, and tyranny of which they form a part.

And all these we must remember have, as a rule, one aim in view; not the production of utilities, but the gaining of a position either for themselves or their children in which they will not have to work at all. It is their ambition and the end of their whole lives to gain, if not for themselves yet at least for their children, the proud position of being obvious burdens on the community.

For their work itself, in spite of the sham dignity with which they surround it, they care nothing: save a few enthusiasts, men of science, art, or letters, who, if they are not the salt of the earth, are at least (and oh, the pity of it!) the salt of the miserable system of which they are the slaves, which hinders and thwarts them at every turn, and even sometimes corrupts them.

Here then is another class, this time very numerous and all-powerful, which produces very little and consumes enormously, and is therefore in the main supported, as paupers are, by the real producers. The class that remains to be considered produces all that is produced, and supports both itself and the other classes, though it is placed in a position of inferiority to them; real inferiority, mind you, involving a degradation both of mind and body.

But it is a necessary consequence of this tyranny and folly that again many of these workers are not producers. A vast number of them once more are merely parasites of property, some of them openly so, as the soldiers by land and sea who are kept on foot for the perpetuating of national rivalries and enmities, and for the purposes of the national struggle for the share of the product of unpaid labour. But besides this obvious burden on the producers and the scarcely less obvious one of domestic servants, there is first the army of clerks, shop-assistants, and so forth, who are engaged in the service of the private war for wealth, which, as above said, is the real occupation of the well-to-do middle class.

This is a larger body of workers than might be supposed, for it includes among others all those engaged in what I should call competitive salesmanship, or, to use a less dignified word, the puffery of wares, which has now got to such a pitch that there are many things which cost far more to sell than they do to make.

Next there is the mass of people employed in making all those articles of folly and luxury, the demand for which is the outcome of the existence of the rich non-producing classes; things which people leading a manly and uncorrupted life would not ask for or dream of. These things, whoever may gainsay me, I will for ever refuse to call wealth: they are not wealth, but waste. Wealth is what nature gives us and what a reasonable man can make out of the gifts of Nature for his reasonable use.

The sunlight, the fresh air, the unspoiled face of the earth, food, raiment, and housing necessary and decent; the storing up of knowledge of all kinds, and the power of disseminating it; means of free communication between man and man; works of art, the beauty which man creates when he is most a man, most aspiring and thoughtful — all things which serve the pleasure of people, free, manly, and uncorrupted. This is wealth. Nor can I think of anything worth having which does not come under one or other of these heads. But think, I beseech you, of the product of England, the workshop of the world, and will you not be bewildered, as I am, at the thought of the mass of things which no sane man could desire, but which our useless toil makes — and sells?

Now, further, there is even a sadder industry yet, which is forced on many, very many, of our workers — the making of wares which are necessary to them and their brethren, *because they are an inferior class.* For if many men live without producing, nay, must live lives so empty and foolish that they *force* a great part of the workers to produce wares which no one needs, not even the rich, it follows that most men must be poor; and, living as they do on wages from those whom they support, cannot get for their use the goods which men naturally desire, but must put up with miserable makeshifts for them, with coarse food that does not nourish, with rotten raiment which does not shelter, with wretched houses which may well make a town-dweller in civilisation look back with regret to the tent of the nomad tribe, or the cave of the pre-historic savage. Nay, the workers must even lend a hand to the great industrial invention of the age — adulteration, and by its help produce for their own use shams and mockeries of the luxury of the rich; for the wage-earners must always live as the wage-payers bid them, and their very habits of life are *forced* on them by their masters.

But it is a waste of time to try to express in words due contempt of the production of the much-praised cheapness of our epoch. It must be enough to say that this cheapness is necessary to the system of exploiting on which modern manufacture rests. In other words, our society includes a great mass of slaves, who must be fed, clothed, housed, and amused as slaves, and that their daily necessity compels them to make the slave-wares whose use is the perpetuation of their slavery.

To sum up, then, concerning the manner of work in civilised States, these States are composed of three classes — a class which does not even pretend to work, a class which pretends to work but which produces nothing, and a class which works, but is compelled by the other two classes to do work which is often unproductive.

Civilisation therefore wastes its own resources, and will do so as long as the present system lasts. These are cold words with which to describe the tyranny under which we suffer; try then to consider what they mean.

There is a certain amount of natural material and of natural forces in the world, and a certain amount of labour-power inherent in the persons of the men that inhabit it. Men urged by their necessities and desires have laboured for many thousands of years at the task of subjugating the forces of Nature and of making the natural material useful to them. To our eyes, since we cannot see into the future, that struggle with Nature seems nearly over, and the victory of the human race over her nearly complete. And, looking backwards to the time when history first began, we note that the progress of that victory has been far swifter and more startling within the last two hundred years than ever before. Surely, therefore, we moderns ought to be in all ways vastly better off than any who have gone before us. Surely we ought, one and all of us, to be wealthy, to be well furnished with the good things which our victory over Nature has won for us.

But what is the real fact? Who will dare to deny that the great mass of civilised men are poor? So poor are they that it is mere childishness troubling ourselves to discuss whether perhaps they are in some ways a little better off than their forefathers. They are poor; nor can their poverty be measured by the poverty of a resourceless savage, for he knows of nothing else than his poverty; that he should be cold, hungry, houseless, dirty, ignorant, all that is to him as natural as that he should have a skin. But for us, for the most of us, civilisation has bred desires which she forbids us to satisfy, and so is not merely a niggard but a torturer also.

Thus then have the fruits of our victory over Nature been stolen from us, thus has compulsion by Nature to labour in hope of rest, gain, and pleasure been turned into compulsion by man to labour in hope — of living to labour!

What shall we do then, can we mend it?

Well, remember once more that it is not our remote ancestors who achieved the victory over Nature, but our fathers, nay, our very selves. For us to sit hopeless and helpless then would be a strange folly indeed: be sure that we can amend it. What, then, is the first thing to be done?

We have seen that modern society is divided into two classes, one of which is *privileged* to be kept by the labour of the other — that is, it forces the other to work for it and takes from this inferior class everything that it *can* take from it, and uses the wealth so taken to keep its own members in a superior position, to make them beings of a higher order than the others: longer lived, more beautiful, more honoured, more refined than those of the other class.

I do not say that it troubles itself about its members being *positively* long lived, beautiful or refined, but merely insists that they shall be so relatively to the inferior class. As also it cannot use the labour-power of the inferior class fairly in producing real wealth, it wastes it wholesale in the production of rubbish.

It is this robbery and waste on the part of the minority which keeps the majority poor; if it could be shown that it is necessary for the preservation of society that this should be submitted to, little more could be said on the matter, save that the despair of the oppressed majority would probably at some time or other destroy society. But it has been shown, on the contrary, even by such incomplete experiments, for instance, as cooperation (so called), that the existence of a privileged class is by no means necessary for the production of wealth, but rather for the 'government' of the producers of wealth, or, in other words, for the upholding of privilege.

The first step to be taken then is to abolish a class of men privileged to shirk their duties as men, thus forcing others to do the work which they refuse to do. All must work according to their ability, and so produce what they consume — that is, each man should work as well as he can for his own livelihood, and his livelihood should be assured to him; that is to say, all the advantages which society would provide for each and all of its members.

Thus, at last, would true society be founded. It would rest on equality of condition. No man would be tormented for the benefit of another — nay, no one man would be tormented for the benefit of society. Nor, indeed, can that order be called society which is not upheld for the benefit of every one of its members.

But since men live now, badly as they live, when so many people do not produce at all, and when so much work is wasted, it is clear that, under conditions where all produced and no work was wasted, not only would everyone work with the certain hope of gaining a due share of wealth by his work, but also he could not miss his due share of rest.

Here, then, are two out of the three kinds of hope mentioned above as an essential part of worthy work assured to the worker. When class robbery is abolished, every man will reap the fruits of his labour, every man will have due rest — leisure, that is. Some socialists might say we need not go any further than this; it is enough that the worker should get the full produce of his work, and that his rest should be abundant. But though the compulsion of men's tyranny is thus abolished, I yet demand compensation for the compulsion of Nature's necessity. As long as the work is repulsive it will still be a burden which must be taken up daily, and even so would mar our life, even though the hours of labour were short. What we want to do is to add to our wealth without diminishing our pleasure. Nature will not be finally conquered till our work becomes a part of the pleasure of our lives.

That first step of freeing people from the compulsion to labour needlessly will at least put us on the way towards this happy end; for we shall then have time and opportunities for bringing it about. As things are now, between the waste of labour-power in mere idleness and its waste in unproductive work, it is clear that the world of civilisation is supported by a small part of its people; when *all* were working usefully for its support, the share of work which each would have to do would be but small, if our standard of life were about on the footing of what well-to-do and refined people now think desirable. We shall have labour-power to spare, and shall in short, be as wealthy as we please. It will be easy to live.

If we were to wake up some morning now, under our present system, and find it "easy to live," that system would force us to set to work at once and make it hard to live; we should call that 'developing our resources', or some such fine name. The multiplication of labour has become a necessity for us, and as long as that goes on no ingenuity in the invention of machines will be of any real use to us. Each new machine will cause a certain amount of misery among the workers whose special industry it may disturb; so many of them will be reduced from skilled to unskilled workmen, and then gradually matters will slip into their due grooves, and all will work apparently smoothly again; and if it were not that all this is preparing revolution, things would be, for the greater part of men, just as they were before the new wonderful invention.

But when revolution has made it "easy to live," when all are working harmoniously together and there is no one to rob the worker of his time, that is to say, his life; in those coming days there will be no compulsion on us to go on producing things we do not want, no compulsion on us to labour for nothing; we shall be able calmly and thoughtfully to consider what we shall do with our wealth of labour-power. Now, for my part, I think the first use we ought to make of that wealth, of that freedom, should be to make all our labour, even the commonest and most necessary, pleasant to everybody; for thinking over the matter carefully I can see that the one course which will certainly make life happy in the face of all accidents and troubles is to take a pleasurable interest in all the details of life.

And lest perchance you think that an assertion too universally accepted to be worth making, let me remind you how entirely modern civilisation forbids it; with what sordid, and even terrible, details it surrounds the life of the poor, what a mechanical and empty life she forces on the rich; and how rare a holiday it is for any of us to feel ourselves a part of Nature, and unhurriedly, thoughtfully, and happily to note the course of our lives amidst all the little links of events which connect them with the lives of others, and build up the great whole of humanity.

But such a holiday our whole lives might be, if we were resolute to make all our labour reasonable and pleasant. But we must be resolute indeed; for no half measures will help us here. It has been said already that our present joyless labour, and our lives scared and anxious as the life of a hunted beast, are forced upon us by the present system of producing for the profit of the privileged classes. It is necessary to state what this means.

Under the present system of wages and capital the "manufacturer" (most absurdly so called, since a manufacturer means a person who makes with his hands) having a monopoly of the means whereby the power to labour inherent in every man's body can be used for production, is the master of those who are not so privileged; he, and he alone, is able to make use of this labour-power, which, on the other hand, is the only commodity by means of which his "capital," that is to say, the accumulated product of past labour, can be made productive to him.

He therefore buys the labour-power of those who are bare of capital and can only live by selling it to him; his purpose in this transaction is to increase his capital, to make it breed.

It is clear that if he paid those with whom he makes his bargain the full value of their labour, that is to say, all that they produced, he would fail in his purpose.

But since he is the monopolist of the means of productive labour, he can *compel* them to make a bargain better for him and worse for them than that; which bargain is that after they have earned their livelihood, estimated according to a standard high enough to ensure their peaceable submission to his mastership, the rest (and by far the larger part as a matter of fact) of what they produce shall belong to him, shall be his *property* to do as he likes with, to use or abuse at his pleasure; which property is, as we all know, jealously guarded by army and navy, police and prison; in short, by that huge mass of physical force which superstition, habit, fear of death by starvation — IGNORANCE, in one word, among the propertyless masses enables the propertied classes to use for the subjection of — their slaves.

Now, at other times, other evils resulting from this system may be put forward. What I want to point out now is the impossibility of our attaining to attractive labour under this system, and to repeat that it is this robbery (there is no other word for it) which wastes the available labour-power of the civilised world, forcing many men to do nothing, and many, very many more to do nothing useful, and forcing those who carry on really useful labour to most burdensome overwork.

For understand once for all that the "manufacturer" aims primarily at producing, by means of the labour he has stolen from others, not goods but profits, that is, the "wealth" that is produced over and above the livelihood of his workmen, and the wear and tear of his machinery. Whether that "wealth" is real or sham matters nothing to him. If it sells and yields him a "profit" it is all right. I have said that, owing to there being rich people who have more money than they can spend reasonably, and who therefore buy sham wealth, there is waste on that side; and also that, owing to there being poor people who cannot afford to buy things which are worth making, there is waste on that side. So that the "demand" which the capitalist "supplies" is a false demand. The market in which he sells is 'rigged' by the miserable inequalities produced by the robbery of the system of Capital and Wages.

It is this system, therefore, which we must be resolute in getting rid of, if we are to attain to happy and useful work for all. The first step towards making labour attractive is to get the means of making labour fruitful, the capital, including the land, machinery, factories, etc., so that we might all work at "supplying" the real "demands" of each and all — that is to say, work for livelihood, instead of working for profit — i.e., the power of compelling other men to work against their will.

When this first step has been taken and men begin to understand that Nature wills all men either to work or starve, and when they are no longer such fools as to allow some the alternative of stealing, when this happy day is come, we shall then be relieved from the tax of waste, and consequently shall find that we have, as aforesaid, a mass of labour-power available, which will enable us to live as we please within reasonable limits. We shall no longer be hurried and driven by the fear of starvation, which at present presses no less on the greater part of men in civilised communities than it does on mere savages. The first and most obvious necessities will be so easily provided for in a community in which there is no waste of labour, that we shall have time to look round and consider what we really do want, that can be obtained without overtaxing our energies; for the often-expressed fear of mere idleness falling upon us when the force supplied by the present hierarchy of compulsion is withdrawn is a fear which is but generated by the burden of excessive and repulsive labour, which we most of us have to bear at present.

I say once more that, in my belief, the first thing which we shall think so necessary as to be worth sacrificing some idle time for, will be the attractiveness of labour. No very heavy sacrifice will be required for attaining this object, but some *will* be required. For we may hope that men who have just waded through a period of strife and revolution will be the last to put up long with a life of mere utilitarianism, though socialists are sometimes accused by ignorant persons of aiming at such a life. On the other hand, the ornamental part of modern life is already rotten to the core, and must be utterly swept away before the new order of things is realised. There is nothing of it — there is nothing which could come of it that could satisfy the aspiration of men set free from the tyranny of commercialism.

We must begin to build up the ornamental part of life — its pleasures, bodily and mental, scientific and artistic, social and individual — on the basis of work undertaken willingly and cheerfully, with the consciousness of benefiting ourselves and our neighbours by it. Such absolutely necessary work as we should have to do would in the first place take up but a small part of each day, and so far would not be burdensome; but it would be a task of daily recurrence, and therefore would spoil our day's pleasure unless it were made at least endurable while it lasted. In other words, all labour, even the commonest, must be made attractive.

How can this be done? — is the question, the answer to which will take up the rest of this paper. In giving some hints on this question, I know that, while all socialists will agree with many of the suggestions made, some of them may seem to some strange and venturesome. These must be considered as being given without any intention of dogmatising, and as merely expressing my own personal opinion.

From all that has been said already it follows that labour, to be attractive, must be directed towards some obviously useful end, unless in cases where it is undertaken voluntarily by each individual as a pastime. This element of obvious usefulness is all the more to be counted on in sweetening tasks otherwise irksome, since social morality, the responsibility of man towards the life of man, will, in the new order of things, take the place of theological morality, or the responsibility of man to some abstract idea. Next, the day's work will be short. This need not be insisted on. It is clear that with work unwasted it can be short. It is clear also that much work which is now a torment, would be easily endurable if it were much shortened.

Variety of work is the next point, and a most important one. To compel a man to do day after day the same task, without any hope of escape or change, means nothing short of turning his life into prison-torment. Nothing but the tyranny of profit-grinding makes this necessary. A man might easily learn and practise at least three crafts, varying sedentary occupation with outdoor occupation calling for the exercise of strong bodily energy for work in which the mind had more to do.

There are few men, for instance, who would not wish to spend part of their lives in the most necessary and pleasantest of all work — cultivating the earth. One thing which will make this variety of employment possible will be the form that education will take in a socially ordered community. At present all education is directed towards the end of fitting people to take their places in the hierarchy of commerce — these as masters, those as workmen.

The education of the masters is more ornamental than that of the workmen, but it is commercial still; and even at the ancient universities learning is but little regarded, unless it can in the long run be made to pay. Due education is a totally different thing from this, and concerns itself in finding out what different people are fit for, and helping them along the road which they are inclined to take. In a duly ordered society, therefore, young people would be taught such handicrafts as they had a turn for as a part of their education, the discipline of their minds and bodies; and adults would also have opportunities of learning in the same schools, for the development of individual capacities would be of all things chiefly aimed at by education, instead, as now, the subordination of all capacities to the great end of 'money-making' for oneself — or one's master. The amount of talent, and even genius, which the present system crushes, and which would be drawn out by such a system, would make our daily work easy and interesting.

Under this head of variety I will note one product of industry which has suffered so much from commercialism that it can scarcely be said to exist, and is, indeed, so foreign from our epoch that I fear there are some who will find it difficult to understand what I have to say on the subject, which I nevertheless must say, since it is really a most important one. I mean that side of art which is, or ought to be, done by the ordinary workman while he is about his ordinary work, and which has got to be called, very properly, Popular Art. This art, I repeat, no longer exists now, having been killed by commercialism. But from the beginning of man's contest with Nature till the rise of the present capitalistic system, it was alive, and generally flourished. While it lasted, everything that was made by man was adorned by man, just as everything made by Nature is adorned by her.

The craftsman, as he fashioned the thing he had under his hand, ornamented it so naturally and so entirely without conscious effort, that it is often difficult to distinguish where the mere utilitarian part of his work ended and the ornamental began. Now the origin of this art was the necessity that the workman felt for variety in his work, and though the beauty produced by this desire was a great gift to the world, yet the obtaining variety and pleasure in the work by the workman was a matter of more importance still, for it stamped all labour with the impress of pleasure. All this has now quite disappeared from the work of civilisation. If you wish to have ornament, you must pay specially for it, and the workman is compelled to produce ornament, as he is to produce other wares. He is compelled to pretend happiness in his work, so that the beauty produced by man's hand, which was once a solace to his labour, has now become an extra burden to him, and ornament is now but one of the follies of useless toil, and perhaps not the least irksome of its fetters.

Besides the short duration of labour, its conscious usefulness, and the variety which should go with it, there is another thing needed to make it attractive, and that is pleasant surroundings. The misery and squalor which we people of civilisation bear with so much complacency as a necessary part of the manufacturing system, is just as necessary to the community at large as a proportionate amount of filth would be in the house of a private rich man.

If such a man were to allow the cinders to be raked all over his drawing- room, and a privy to be established in each corner of his dining- room, if he habitually made a dust and refuse heap of his once beautiful garden, never washed his sheets or changed his tablecloth, and made his family sleep five in a bed, he would surely find himself in the claws of a commission *de lunatico.*

But such acts of miserly folly are just what our present society is doing daily under the compulsion of a supposed necessity, which is nothing short of madness. I beg you to bring your commission of lunacy against civilisation without more delay.

For all our crowded towns and bewildering factories are simply the outcome of the profit system. Capitalistic manufacture, capitalistic land-owning, and capitalistic exchange force men into big cities in order to manipulate them in the interests of capital; the same tyranny contracts the due space of the factory so much that (for instance) the interior of a great weaving-shed is almost as ridiculous a spectacle as it is a horrible one. There is no other necessity for all this, save the necessity for grinding profits out of men's lives, and of producing cheap goods for the use (and subjection) of the slaves who grind. All labour is not yet driven into factories; often where it is there is no necessity for it, save again the profit-tyranny. People engaged in all such labour need by no means be compelled to pig together in close city quarters. There is no reason why they should not follow their occupations in quiet country homes, in industrial colleges, in small towns, or, in short, where they find it happiest for them to live.

As to that part of labour which must be associated on a large scale, this very factory system, under a reasonable order of things (though to my mind there might still be drawbacks to it), would at least offer opportunities for a full and eager social life surrounded by many pleasures. The factories might be centres of intellectual activity also, and work in them might well be varied very much: the tending of the necessary machinery might to each individual be but a short part of the day's work. The other work might vary from raising food from the surrounding country to the study and practice of art and science.

It is a matter of course that people engaged in such work, and being the masters of their own lives, would not allow any hurry or want of foresight to force them into enduring dirt, disorder, or want of room. Science duly applied would enable them to get rid of refuse, to minimise, if not wholly to destroy, all the inconveniences which at present attend the use of elaborate machinery, such as smoke, stench, and noise; nor would they endure that the buildings in which they worked or lived should be ugly blots on the fair face of the earth. Beginning by making their factories, buildings, and sheds decent and convenient like their homes, they would infallibly go on to make them not merely negatively good, inoffensive merely, but even beautiful, so that the glorious art of architecture, now for some time slain by commercial greed, would be born again and flourish.

So, you see, I claim that work in a duly ordered community should be made attractive by the consciousness of usefulness, by its being carried on with intelligent interest, by variety, and by its being exercised amidst pleasurable surroundings. But I have also claimed, as we all do, that the day's work should not be wearisomely long. It may be said, "How can you make this last claim square with the others? If the work is to be so refined, will not the goods made be very expensive?"

I do admit, as I have said before, that some sacrifice will be necessary in order to make labour attractive. I mean that, if we could be contented in a free community to work in the same hurried, dirty, disorderly, heartless way as we do now, we might shorten our day's labour very much more than I suppose we shall do, taking all kinds of labour into account. But if we did, it would mean that our new-won freedom of condition would leave us listless and wretched, if not anxious, as we are now, which I hold necessary for raising our condition to the standard called out for as desirable by the whole community.

Nor only so. We should, individually, be tremulous to sacrifice quite freely still more of our time and our ease towards the raising of the standard of life. Persons, either by themselves or associated for such purposes, would freely, and for the love of the work and for its results — stimulated by the hope of the pleasure of creation — produce those ornaments of life for the service of all, which they are now bribed to produce (or pretend to produce) for the service of a few rich men.

The experiment of a civilised community living wholly without art or literature has not yet been tried. The past degradation and corruption of civilisation may force this denial of pleasure upon the society which will arise from its ashes. If that must be, we will accept the passing phase of utilitarianism as a foundation for the art which is to be. If the cripple and the starveling disappear from our streets, if the earth nourish us all alike, if the sun shine for all of us alike, if to one and all of us the glorious drama of the earth — day and night, summer and winter — can be presented as a thing to understand and love, we can afford to wait awhile till we are purified from the shame of the past corruption, and till art arises again amongst people freed from the terror of the slave and the shame of the robber.

Meantime, in any case, the refinement, thoughtfulness, and deliberation of labour must indeed be paid for, but not by compulsion to labour long hours. Our epoch has invented machines which would have appeared wild dreams to the men of past ages, and of those machines we have as yet *made no use.*

They are called "labour-saving" machines — a commonly used phrase which implies what we expect of them; but we do not get what we expect. What they really do is to reduce the skilled labourer to the ranks of the unskilled, to increase the number of the 'reserve army of labour' — that is, to increase the precariousness of life among the workers and to intensify the labour of those who serve the machines (as slaves their masters). All this they do by the way, while they pile up the profits of the employers of labour, or force them to expend those profits in bitter commercial war with each other. In a true society these miracles of ingenuity would be for the first time used for minimizing the amount of time spent in unattractive labour, which by their means might be so reduced as to be but a very light burden on each individual.

All the more as these machines would most certainly be very much improved when it was no longer a question as to whether their improvement would 'pay' the individual, but rather whether it would benefit the community.

So much for the ordinary use of machinery, which would probably, after a time, be somewhat restricted when men found out that there was no need for anxiety as to mere subsistence, and learned to take an interest and pleasure in handiwork which, done deliberately and thoughtfully, could be made more attractive than machine work.

Again, as people freed from the daily terror of starvation find out what they really wanted, being no longer compelled by anything but their own needs, they would refuse to produce the mere inanities which are now called luxuries, or the poison and trash now called cheap wares. No-one would make plush breeches when there were no flunkies to wear them, nor would anybody waste his time over making oleomargarine when no one was *compelled* to abstain from real butter. Adulteration laws are only needed in a society of thieves — and in such a society they are a dead letter.

Socialists are often asked how work of the rougher and more repulsive kind could be carried out in the new condition of things. To attempt to answer such questions fully or authoritatively would be attempting the impossibility of constructing a scheme of a new society out of the materials of the old, before we knew which of those materials would disappear and which endure through the evolution which is leading us to the great change.

Yet it is not difficult to conceive of some arrangement whereby those who did the roughest work should work for the shortest spells. And again, what is said above of the variety of work applies specially here. Once more I say, that for a man to be the whole of his life hopelessly engaged in performing one repulsive and never-ending task, is an arrangement fit enough for the hell imagined by theologians, but scarcely fit for any other form of society. Lastly, if this rougher work were of any special kind, we may suppose that special volunteers would be called on to perform it, who would surely be forthcoming, unless men in a state of freedom should lose the sparks of manliness which they possessed as slaves.

And yet if there be any work which cannot be made other than repulsive, either by the shortness of its duration or the intermittency of its recurrence, or by the sense of special and peculiar usefulness (and therefore honour) in the mind of the man who performs it freely — if there be any work which cannot be but a torment to the worker, what then? Well, then, let us see if the heavens will fall on us if we leave it undone, for it were better that they should.

The produce of such work cannot be worth the price of it.

Now we have seen that the semi-theological dogma that all labour, under any circumstances, is a blessing to the labourer, is hypocritical and false; that, on the other hand, labour is good when due hope of rest and pleasure accompanies it. We have weighed the work of civilisation in the balance and found it wanting, since hope is mostly lacking to it, and therefore we see that civilisation has bred a dire curse for men. But we have seen also that the work of the world might be carried on in hope and with pleasure if it were not wasted by folly and tyranny, by the perpetual strife of opposing classes.

It is peace, therefore, which we need in order that we may live and work in hope and with pleasure. Peace so much desired, if we must trust men's words, but which has been so continually and steadily rejected by them in deeds. But for us, let us set our hearts on it and win it at whatever cost.

What the cost may be, who can tell? Will it be possible to win peace peaceably? Alas, how can it be? We are so hemmed in by wrong and folly, that in one way or other we must always be fighting against them: our own lives may see no end to the struggle, perhaps no obvious hope of the end. It may be that the best we can hope to see is that struggle getting sharper and bitterer day by day, until it breaks out openly at last into the slaughter of man by actual warfare instead of by the slower and crueller methods of 'peaceful' commerce.

If we live to see that, we shall live to see much, for it will mean the rich classes grown conscious of their own wrong and robbery, and, consciously defending them by open violence; and then the end will be drawing near.

But in any case, and whatever the nature of our strife for peace may be, if we only aim at it steadily and with singleness of heart, and ever keep it in view, a reflection from that peace of the future will illumine the turmoil and trouble of our lives, whether the trouble be seemingly petty, or obviously tragic; and we shall, in our hopes at least, live the lives of men: nor can the present times give us any reward greater than that.

# THE PROBLEM OF WORK

## THE TYRANNY OF THE CLOCK

*George Woodcock*

*Woodcock (1912-1995) was a well-known poet, essayist and critic from Canada, who founded the journal* Canadian Literature. *He was a member of the Freedom Press editorial group from 1941-49 and published several books with the collective. This article was first published in* War Commentary *in March 1944.*

In no characteristic is existing society in the West so sharply distinguished from the earlier societies, whether of Europe or the East, than in its conception of time. To the ancient Chinese or Greek, to the Arab herdsman or Mexican peon of today, time is represented in the cyclic processes of nature, the alternation of day and night, the passage from season to season. The nomads and farmers measured and still measure their day from sunrise to sunset, and their year in terms of seedtime and harvest, of the falling leaf and the ice thawing on the lakes and rivers. The farmer worked according to the elements, the craftsman for so long as he felt it necessary to perfect his product. Time was seen in a process of natural change, and men were not concerned in its exact measurement.

For this reason civilisations highly developed in other respects had the most primitive means of measuring time, the hour glass with its trickling sand or dripping water, the sundial, useless on a dull day, and the candle or lamp whose unburnt remnant of oil or wax indicated the hours. All these devices were approximate and inexact, and were often rendered unreliable by the weather or the personal laziness of the tender. Nowhere in the ancient or medieval world were more than a tiny minority of men concerned with time in the terms of mathematical exactitude.

Modern, Western man, however, lives in a world which runs according to the mechanical and mathematical symbols of clock time. The clock dictates his movements and inhibits his actions.

The clock turns time from a process of nature into a commodity that can be measured and bought and sold like soap or sultanas. And because, without some means of exact time keeping, industrial capitalism could never have developed and could not continue to exploit the workers, the clock represents an element of mechanical tyranny in the lives of modern men more potent than any individual exploiter or than any other machine. It is valuable to trace the historical process by which the clock influenced the social development of modern European civilisation.

It is a frequent circumstance of history that a culture or civilisation develops the device that will later be used for its destruction. The ancient Chinese, for example, invented gunpowder, which was developed by the military experts of the West and eventually led to the Chinese civilisation itself being destroyed by the high explosives of modern warfare. Similarly, the supreme achievement of the ingenuity of the craftsmen in the medieval cities of Europe was the invention of the mechanical clock, which, with its revolutionary alteration of the concept of time, materially assisted the growth of exploiting capitalism and the destruction of the medieval culture.

There is a tradition that the clock appeared in the eleventh century, as a device for ringing bells at regular intervals in the monasteries which, with the regimented life they imposed on their inmates, were the closest social approximation in the middle ages to the factory of today. The first authenticated clock, however, appeared in the thirteenth century, and it was not until the fourteenth century that clocks became common as ornaments of the public buildings in the German cities.

These early clocks, operated by weights, were not particularly accurate, and it was not until the sixteenth century that any great reliability was attained. In England, for instance, the clock at Hampton Court, made in 1540, is said to have been the first accurate clock in the country. And even the accuracy of the sixteenth century clocks are relative, for they were equipped only with hour hands. The idea of measuring time in minutes and seconds had been thought out by the early mathematicians as far back as the fourteenth century, but it was not until the invention of the pendulum in 1657 that sufficient accuracy was attained to permit the addition of a minute hand, and the second hand did not appear until the eighteenth century. These two centuries, it should be observed, were those in which capitalism grew to such an extent that it was able to take advantage of the industrial revolution in technique in order to establish its domination over society.

The clock, as Lewis Mumford has pointed out, represents the key machine of the machine age, both for its influence on technics and for its influence on the habits of men. Technically, the clock was the first really automatic machine that attained any importance in the life of men. Previous to its invention, the common machines were of such a nature that their operation depended on some external and unreliable force, such as human or animal muscles, water or wind. It is true that the Greeks had invented a number of primitive automatic machines, but these were used, like Hero's steam engine, either for obtaining "supernatural" effects in the temples or for amusing the tyrants of Levantine cities. But the clock was the first automatic machine that attained a public importance and a social function. Clock-making became the industry from which men learnt the elements of machine making and gained the technical skill that was to produce the complicated machinery of the industrial revolution.

Socially the clock had a more radical influence than any other machine, in that it was the means by which the regularisation and regimentation of life necessary for an exploiting system of industry could best be attained.

The clock provided a means by which time — a category so elusive that no philosophy has yet determined its nature — could be measured concretely in the more tangible terms of space provided by the circumference of a clock dial. Time as duration became disregarded, and men began to talk and think always of "lengths" of time, just as if they were talking of lengths of calico. And time, being now measurable in mathematical symbols, became regarded as a commodity that could be bought and sold in the same way as any other commodity.

The new capitalists, in particular, became rabidly time-conscious. Time, here symbolising the labour of the workers, was regarded by them almost as if it were the chief raw material of industry. "Time is money" became one of the key slogans of capitalist ideology, and the timekeeper was the most significant of the new types of official introduced by the capitalist dispensation.

In the early factories the employers went so far as to manipulate their clocks or sound their factory whistles at the wrong times in order to defraud the workers of a little of this valuable new commodity. Later such practices became less frequent, but the influence of the clock imposed a regularity on the lives of the majority of men which had previously been known only in the monastery. Men actually became like clocks, acting with a repetitive regularity which had no resemblance to the rhythmic life of a natural being. They became as the Victorian phrase put it, "as regular as clockwork." Only in the country districts where the natural lives of animals and plants and the elements still dominated life, did any large proportion of the population fail to succumb to the deadly tick of monotony.

At first this new attitude to time, this new regularity of life, was imposed by the clock-owning masters on the unwilling poor. The factory slave reacted in his spare time by living with a chaotic irregularity which characterised the gin-sodden slums of early nineteenth-century industrialism. Men fled to the timeless world of drink or Methodist inspiration. But gradually the idea of regularity spread downward among the workers. Nineteenth-century religion and morality played their part by proclaiming the sin of "wasting time." The introduction of mass-produced watches and clocks in the 1850's spread time-consciousness among those who had previously merely reacted to the stimulus of the knocker-up or the factory whistle. In the church and the school, in the office and the workshop, punctuality was held up as the greatest of the virtues.

Out of this slavish dependence on mechanical time which spread insidiously into every class in the nineteenth century there grew up the demoralising regimentation of life which characterises factory work today. The man who fails to conform faces social disapproval and economic ruin. If he is late at the factory the worker will lose his job or even, at the present day,* find himself in prison.

* *Woodcock is referring to World War II regulations in force in Britain at the time*

Hurried meals, the regular morning and evening scramble for trains or buses, the strain of having to work to time schedules, all contribute by digestive and nervous disturbance, to ruin health and shorten life.

Nor does the financial imposition of regularity tend, in the long run, to greater efficiency. Indeed, the quality of the product is usually much poorer, because the employer, regarding time as a commodity which he has to pay for, forces the operative to maintain such a speed that his work must necessarily be skimped. Quantity rather than quality becoming the criterion, the enjoyment is taken out of the work itself, and the worker in his turn becomes a 'clock-watcher', concerned only with when he will be able to escape to the scanty and monotonous leisure of industrial society, in which he 'kills time' by cramming in as much time-scheduled and mechanised enjoyment of cinema, radio and newspaper as his wage packet and his tiredness will allow. Only if he is willing to accept the hazards of living by his faith or his wits can the man without money avoid living as a slave to the clock.

The problem of the clock is, in general, similar to that of the machine. Mechanical time is valuable as a means of co-ordination of activities in a highly developed society, just as the machine is valuable as a means of reducing unnecessary labour to a minimum. Both are valuable for the contribution they make to the smooth running of society, and should be used insofar as they assist men to co-operate efficiently and to eliminate monotonous toil and social confusion. But neither should be allowed to dominate men's lives as they do today.

Now the movement of the clock sets the tempo of men's lives — they become the servant of the concept of time which they themselves have made, and are held in fear, like Frankenstein by his own monster. In a sane and free society such an arbitrary domination of man's functions by either clock or machine would obviously be out of the question. The domination of man by the creation of man is even more ridiculous than the domination of man by man. Mechanical time would be relegated to its true function of a means of reference and co-ordination, and men would return again to a balanced view of life no longer dominated by time-regulation and the worship of the clock. Complete liberty implies freedom from the tyranny of abstractions as well as from the rule of men.

# THE PROBLEM OF WORK

*Camillo Berneri*

*Berneri (1897-1937) was a philosopher, anarchist theorist and militant anti-fascist murdered in the Barcelona May Days. This essay was first published in Italian with the title* Il Lavoro Attraente *(Geneva 1938). An English translation was serialised in* Freedom *newspaper in the late '40s. This is a 1983 translation by Vernon Richards, based on the* Freedom *version.*

On this eve of social upheavals and in the midst of so much ranting about state socialism, authoritarian communism and simplistic economics it should be the anarchists' specific task to put the problem of the discipline of work in clear and concrete terms; a problem like any other social problem needs to be updated in accordance with new technical trends, with new economic, physiological and psychological knowledge, as well as with the various problems that are having to be faced as a result of the different tendencies emerging from the ranks of the industrial proletariat.

While keeping to its broad aims and final objective, anarchism must define the means and methods of its future as a new order. What activity is more universal than work? What problem is vaster and more intermingled with all other problems than that of work? Economic, physiological and psychological laws, as well as practically all society and nearly the whole of man's life are involved in this activity, which even today is drudgery, but which tomorrow will become the supreme human dignity.

The essay which follows is a kind of introduction to the theme of "Attractive Work," to which I should like to see the attention drawn of all those who could contribute ideas, personal experience and particular technical knowledge. An expert would have done more and better; but as the experts are usually disinclined to part with their acquired knowledge, it is up to the less inhibited to raise these questions and bring them to the attention of our comrades.

We shall have made a stride forward if, at our meetings and in the press, we are able to analyse the question of free and attractive work, the more so as this problem involves many others and is, by its very nature, likely to recall interesting experiences and to suggest constructive schemes.

## Workers as Slaves

*I have seen the blacksmith at work before the open flame of his forge. His hands were soiled and he was as dirty as a crocodile.*
*The various workers who handle the chisel — do they enjoy more leisure than the peasant? Their field is the wood they carve, and they work well after the day is ended and even at night if there is light in their houses.*

*The mason works the hardest stones. When he has finished carrying out the orders*
*received and his hands are tired, does he perhaps, take a rest? He must be back at the*
*yard at sunrise though his knees and back are at breaking point.*
*The barber works at his trade well into the night. For a mouthful of bread he must run*
*from house to house in search of his customers.*
*Why such toil hardly to fill one's belly?*
*And the dyer of cloth? His hands stink; they smell of putrid fish.*
*His eyes droop with sleep, but his hands never rest from preparing finely-coloured robes.*
*He hates cloth, every kind of cloth.*
*The cobbler is very unhappy, and is always complaining he has nothing to chew but his*
*leather.*
*They work, they all work — but it is as with honey, the gatherer alone eats it.*

This poem, which dates from the fourteenth century before Christ and describes workers' conditions in the reign of Rameses II of Egypt, expresses a lament which continues throughout the centuries. In slave societies, work is a curse. But even apart from its servile state, it is pain and suffering. The repugnance which the shepherd, turned peasant and artisan, has for work, is reflected in the religious dogma which holds that work is a consequence of, and a penance for, an error committed by the first human couple.

The distaste of pastoral and warrior societies for work led to making woman "a domestic animal" and the slave the "typical worker." To the slave, work is nothing but suffering. The negro slave who once said to a traveller: ''The monkey is a very intelligent animal, and could talk if it wanted to; if it does not, that is because it does not want to be forced to work'' — was merely expressing the attitude of the worker to servile labour.

Ancient mythologies depict the tiller of the soil as a reprobate paying for his sins of rebellion: Adam, progenitor of the human race, is the angel fallen from the heaven of idleness to the hell of work.

According to Christian ethics, work is imposed by God on man as a penance consequent on original sin. Ancient and medieval Catholicism glorified work mostly as an expiation of sin. The Reformation, too, considered work as "remedium peccati" although Luther and Calvin went further than Saint Thomas by forecasting the modern conception of the dignity of work, an idea outlined by the major thinkers of the Renaissance.

Bourgeois moralism transferred the principle of work as a duty to the field of civil morals, and invented a mystique whereby the exploited serf was placed on a monument as "knight of labour," the "faithful servant," the "model worker," and so on.

The petty-bourgeois mentality and the stupefying adaptability typical of the artisan, of the craftsman's son turned factory operative and of the townified peasant, were responsible for their lack of deep awareness of the capitalist yoke and the decadence of their own personality. Emile Zola in *Travail* paints a true and convincing picture of the type of dull-witted worker who thinks of the boss as an indispensable provider of work and serves him with doglike fidelity, shuns the struggles for emancipation, regards new discoveries with hostility, and accepts the slavery of work with a fatalistic passivity which soon degenerates into a form of masochism.

The advent of socialist literature, pitying and indignant, finally brought the proletariat to a realisation of its own serfdom. The development of industrialism has been painted in sombre colours by those who have examined it from the point of view of man, not the money-box. Heine, in *What is Germany?* speaks of England as "an abominable country, where machines work like men, and men like machines." Marx and Engels speak of the lives of the workers in their time as a "living hell." Engels depicted the industrial capitalist as a feudalist, and the factory as a gaol: "The slavery which the bourgeoisie have imposed on the proletariat is clearly visible in the factory system. Here all liberty is forfeited, *de jure* and *de facto*. The operative must be at his workshop at dawn; if he is two minutes late he runs the risk of losing his day's pay. He must eat, read and sleep to order. The despotic bell breaks into his slumbers and interrupts his meals."

Not only Marx and Engels but also Lassalle, Lafargue and other socialist writers rise up against this industrial slavery, which they denounce not only as a method of social exploitation, but as a system for the degradation of man. Engels, in his book *On the Position of the Working Classes in England* and Paul Lafargue in his *Property, its Origin and Evolution*, both illustrate the brutishness to which extreme specialisation of work leads.

Bakunin and other anarchist writers took up and further developed this criticism. Peter Kropotkin proclaimed: "The division of work means man classified, stamped and labelled for the rest of his life, making knots in some material, or driving a truck at the minehead, without any general idea of the significance of machine, industry or mine and thereby losing all taste for work and the capacity for inventiveness which had at the inception of modern industrialism, created the mechanical devices of which we are so fond of priding ourselves."

The time when the working day was thirteen hours long, and even sixteen or seventeen hours, has passed; but the monstrous workshops which run on the so-called 'rationalisation of work' method are still with us, as shown, for example, by Egon Erwin Kisch, who describes, in *American Paradise*, workers' conditions in Ford's Detroit factories.

The modern factory worker wears out his brain and nervous system. Boredom, on the other hand, is the inevitable result of automatic work. Tarde, discussing the pathological effects of boredom, asserts that it causes "irregularities of circulation and nutrition, sensibility to cold, diminishing of muscular tone, loss of appetite and weight."

Dr P Janet in his book on neurosis quotes the case of a girl doing a monotonous job, who, to avoid boredom, was in the habit of giving rapid glances out of the window into the road on her left. She slowly developed a nervous tic which made her jerk her head incessantly to the left. The same doctor tells of another girl who was obliged to work far into the night, and, fighting against boredom and sleep, she soon developed a rhythmical 'chorea' (involuntary nervous movement) in which she would turn her right wrist and move her right foot regularly up and down. These movements, performed in a state of somnambulism and accompanied by the words "I must work" spoken out loud, were those of her occupation. She made dolls' eyes and had to operate a lathe, pedalling with the right foot and working a flywheel with the right hand.

I myself, watching typists at work, have noticed that several of them were victims of a nervous tic obviously connected with weariness and boredom.

The present attitude of people to work has been the object of special research. The widespread aversion of the operatives for their occupation, if a monotonous one, is plain from workers' autobiographies collected by Adolf Levenstein (Berlin, 1909). A weaver and a metal worker both express a real loathing for their work. In another investigation carried out by the same author (Munich, 1912) the repugnance of the workers for their jobs is even more evident.

- A mechanic writes: "The moment the bell sounds, I dash like a madman to the doors leading out of the factory."
- A lathe-machinist: "Work is ended for the day. I feel an inward uplift and relaxation and would like to shout for joy," Another says: "I force myself to take an interest in my work, and yet I am unable to." And still another: "Faced with each new day's work, I feel renewed horror growing within me. I cannot imagine how I shall be able to stand ten hours of this martyrdom."
- A metal-worker: "I take no interest whatever in my work, and if by chance on a day off I catch sight of the factory chimneys, I feel as if I had been reminded of something unpleasant." And this frightful view of another worker: "I find no pleasure in my work. I go to work as I would go to my death."
- A weaver says: "Purely and simply, I hate my work."

Arturo Labriola sums up the results of that most interesting enquiry as follows: "1803 replied to the author's questions. Of these, 307 (that is 17%) declared that they found pleasure in their work — but often for reasons indirectly connected with their job, or of a personal nature. 1,027 workers (56.9%) found their work repugnant or even loathsome. 308 persons (17.1%) declared themselves indifferent either way (due to force of habit, because "work was necessary" or because they had never given it any thought). And 161 (9%) gave no reply whatever. In other words, a mere 17% said they were happy in their work; but no one can say whether they were sincere or not. People are influenced by tradition, school training and so on, and tend to give a conventional answer or quote a traditional saying, such as "idleness is the fountain of all evils," etc.

Had the conventional mentality been absent the final results of the enquiry might have been still more revealing; it is nevertheless, a distressing fact that more than 80% of those asked had either a definite loathing for their work, or a concept of work as something mechanical to which they remained passive and silent."

In *Beyond Capitalism and Socialism*, (Paris 1931) Labriola comments on the result of these enquiries as follows:

> Work as such suggests nothing to the worker's mind. It is, to the operative, mere execution — execution of a fragment or a part of a plan. The plan and its practical working-out have nothing to do with the operative. They are the exclusive concern of the contractor and the factory management, who alone take decisions.
>
> In the 'Taylorised' or 'Fordised' high-efficiency factory, the operative does not even understand what purpose his work serves, and he would certainly be quite incapable of recognising in the finished product the part to which his own work had contributed.
>
> Work of this nature, therefore, can only mean either disgust and boredom to the worker or nothing at all — indeed, better for him if his function should become entirely automatic, producing in him such a degree of insensiblity as will help him forget the burden of his labour.

Labriola, as is wont with him and other pessimists, tends to generalise; but what he says is certainly true for the majority of workers in large industries. I have with me a collection of poems written by French, English and American workers, and they all evince the same complaint: the sequence of interminable days, the weariness that annihilates thought, the desire to escape from the daily round, the terror at the thought that the whole of life will be like yesterday and today. To the production lines are now added the piece-work systems which accentuate the robot-like nature of industrial work. A Turin worker gives the following example of the Bedaux system (*The Workers' State*, Paris August, 1933):

> A worker has to make a certain metal part. He is given 30 seconds to complete this operation, divided into two, first the rough approximation, then the finishing. To do this he must shift the machine's roller four times. But while the lathe is doing one part of the job, he must go to the drill-press and fix a grummet to it. Then he returns to the lathe, takes out the turned piece and puts another in position, then he goes to the drill with the piece from the lathe. He therefore has to work two lathes and a drill, and all his movements at the various machines and in passing from one to the other are timed with the utmost precision. He cannot delay for one second or he will damage one or another of the perforating or turning equipment, and if this happens his wage will be insufficient to pay for the damage, apart from the threat of dismissal. It is easy to understand in what state this worker will be at the end of his working day.

In the same enquiry a "worker of a large factory" described the system as follows:

> The Bedaux system begins with an office consisting of engineers, time-keepers and workers with long experience.

All materials used are rigorously examined and catalogued by this department. Tables are made out showing the various qualities of the steel used; metric speeds of working are decided on; the machines are studied with a view to determining how many movements and operations can be carried out with them in a given time.

"The allocation of machines is now done differently — previously the best machine was entrusted to the most accurate worker; whereas today the machine goes to the strongest or most useful man according to qualities of the machine itself. All the necessary tools are no longer available to each individual worker that he may use them according to his capabilities; their type and number are unalterably fixed according to the job-sheet which accompanies the item to be manufactured.

Every physical movement of which an operative is capable is calculated and transformed into 'bedaux,' that is, working time. Here is an example taken from a job-sheet:

"Operations: lathe No.1, 39 revs., advance 0.25, tool C.15, Bedaux 0.33; lathe No.2, revs., 40, advance 0.15, tool G.l3, Bedaux 0.15. Total Bedaux, 0.48.

"This means that the piece must be completed in 48 seconds. The very sight of these figures puts fear into the operative. He starts to make the piece. When it is completed, he realises that instead of 48 seconds, it has taken him 1 min. 10 seconds ("Bedaux").

"Then the Bedaux office intervenes: the worker is told to give a further demonstration in the presence of the time-keepers, who refer to the appropriate index-card (which is kept in the office like a record of criminals), his movements are watched and corrected where wrong; this done, the Bedaux office 'expert' carries out the operation.

"First, everything is once more checked: machine number, components, tools, etc. The operative is told to observe the 'demonstrator's' movements, especially where the left hand supplements the right, the bending of the body, the leg movements and so on. The task of the 'demonstrator' is, basically to convince the operative that he must become automatic, himself a piece of mechanism.

It sometimes happens that even after the demonstration the worker does very little better — instead of 1 minute 10 seconds per piece, he has taken, say, 1 min. 5 secs. — he is still a long way from 0.48! In this case his replacement is inevitable, and he is either put to work on a simpler machine or else he is dismissed from the factory. Another worker may take 1.10 'bedaux' the first time, the second 0.59, the third he may reach 0.48; indeed, his work becomes an exercise, familiarity provides training, and from 0.48 he drops to 0.40.

"In this case he does not benefit by the 0.08 'bedaux' gained; his share is only three-quarters, the other quarter going to the technical department!

A prize is given to those operatives who call attention to a superfluous movement and the secrecy of their suggestion is guaranteed by the management. The Bedaux system is applied, in some factories, in more or less elastic form, but the fact remains that if the technical office is made up of expert engineers, the workers will be turned into automatons during their working hours."

The "worker of a large factory" concludes thus:

> The Bedaux system is in fact a method of work-intensification pushed to the limit. The workers employed in factories where this system is used must be strong and healthy. All calculations of labour-power, resting-time and so on are based on a worker 'in perfect condition'; consequently, the elderly are eliminated, and those whose health is not perfect are obliged to pass these workshops by, for even were they to be tolerated, their wages would be negligible.
>
> All applied systems of organised production, and every new mechanical device, have brought, under the capitalist regime, only an increase in exploitation, accompanied by an increase in unemployment. The Bedaux system burdens still further the workers' conditions. The greatest efforts he can make are demanded of the worker — all he gives is stolen from him.
>
> The system creates a class of workers who are practically robots. They work at terrific speed. They are soon exhausted — physical wrecks — and waiting to be thrown out, but in the meantime the existence of this stratum of workers brings with it a progressive increase in the exploitation of the whole working-class, because it acts as a stimulus to the refining of the technique of exploitation. In the last analysis what is developed more and more is working-class poverty.

To the mechanisation of the worker must be added the increasing number of accidents, spreading a feeling of dejection in the workshops, yards and mines.

Industrial work today is inhuman. It is a Moloch which crushes with weariness and boredom, which squeezes the worker and then spits him out, prematurely aged; which throws him on to the street or chains him to servitude; which wounds when it does not cripple or kill.

Considering the conditions under which they toil, there is reason to marvel that there are so few who escape from their industrial prisons by banditry, vagrancy or some other way; and it is humiliating to note that there are relatively few who, by means of strikes, sabotage and other methods of struggle, try to blow the altar of Mammon sky-high.

A young teacher at an industrial school in Northern France gave the following thought by Jean-Richard Bloch to his pupils as a subject for an essay: "If the factory aspires to be not only a place of physical work but also a place of dignity, pride and happiness, it is clear that it must lose any resemblance to what we call 'factory' in our own countries."

J R Bloch, to whom the teacher sent a selection of these essays, has picked out some significant passages (*Europe*, Paris, June, 1934).

Nearly all these sons of workers, living in an over-industrialised region, stress the brutality of bosses and foremen, and the ugliness of the factories. One of them writes: "The directors should understand that they will not get men to do good work by behaving brutally towards them."

Another says: "That which wounds the worker most is the contempt with which he is treated." Nearly all the pupils expressed disgust at the "foul smell," the "workshops filthy with grease," the "factory walls black with soot." They contrast the factory they see with the 'ideal' factory, which will be the 'real' factory in the not too distant future.

## Pleasant Work

"In the ideal workshop," writes one of these children, "the foreman distributes the work to the operatives in the morning and talks to them as equals. They are not heard yelling and swearing at the workers, as is the case at present. The manager, for his part, is careful not to offend the works-foremen with orders."

All the pupils, too, portray the ideal factory as being situated in the country. They all visualise light-coloured walls, they all speak of sun, light, health. The workshops will be cooled in summer, warmed in winter, for "human nature has need of a minimum of well-being to remain good."

Another says: "A worker will enter a factory of this kind as if he were entering his own home. There will be washing facilities, that he may leave the factory as clean as he entered it. He will be proud of his factory; when he passes by it with a friend, he will say, 'This is the factory where I work,' and as he will be happy in his work this will lead to a happy family life." Nearly all furnish this imaginary place with practical means of communication, and nearly all dream of libraries, recreation-rooms, etc.

These remarks are by children who have read neither Kropotkin's *Conquest of Bread* nor Zola's *Travail*, nor yet the futuristic anticipations of William Morris and Bellamy; and yet the bright dream still flourishes, for it is the workers' aspiration on the threshold of a new era.

The idea of attractive work is a very ancient one. We find it clearly expressed in *The Works and Days* of Hesiod, the Greek poet who lived eight or nine centuries before Christ. The formula "Do what you will" as applied to work, is one of the characteristics of the life of the Thelemites expressed by Rabelais in the sixteenth century (*Gargantua* Chap. 57). Fenelon in the third book of the *Telemachus* (1699) also applies this formula to work. Morelly, in *Basiliade* wrote: "In admitting that man's free activity pours into the common pool more than his needs take out of it, it is clear that laws and regulations become practically worthless, for every necessary function corresponds in the individual to a natural taste, a well-defined vocation. The leaders' opinions will be accepted with pleasure; no one will think himself dispensed from work which a unanimous and collective effort will render varied and attractive.

Nothing would be easier to regulate than a fraternal concourse of this kind, since from the most enlightened freedom would result the most perfect order."

It was Fourier who amply and systematically developed the principle of attractive work, the first condition of which is — according to him — variety; and the second, brevity of duration — "pleasant and effortless" work is one of the socialist achievements foretold in Cabet's Voyage en Icarie (1840).

Victor Considerant, who was the champion and elaborator of the idea of attractive work, was right when he told M Lausac (*Plus Loin*, Paris, July, 1933) that among Fourier's conceptions, the notion of "attractive work" for groups or individuals would be one of those receiving greatest attention from future generations — Benoit Malon, Georges Renard, Jean Jaures and other French socialists were clearly influenced by Fourier's conception of the organisation of work. Emile Zola in his novel *Travail* shows us a factory where varied work, carried out in clean and well-lighted surroundings and aided by machines, has become a "recreation, a joy and a real pleasure." Zola gives us a fundamental principle, an act of faith and a sure prophecy that work shall become "the law of life itself."

Some nineteenth-century physiologists have also maintained the possibility of attractive work. One of these — Rossi-Doria — wrote in one of his reports that "Work must no longer be a torment and a source of ills, but a joy and an important factor in physical and moral health."

The anarchist writers in particular have contributed in keeping alive the idea of attractive work. Peter Kropotkin makes this categorical affirmation: "In collective work, carried out with gay spirit to reach the desired goal — be it book, work of art or luxury article — each one will find the stimulus, the uplift necessary to make life pleasant."

When, in our writings and speeches, we predict that the day will come when all, or nearly all, will work spontaneously and with pleasure, frequently comes the reply, "It is a Utopian dream!" Nevertheless, there are men in our society today who work longer hours without weariness; with, on the contrary, a deep sense of satisfaction. These are the scientists, the thinkers, and the artists.

I have in front of me some very interesting replies to an enquiry made by the *Philosophical and Allied Sciences Review* of 1907. Here are a few of them: Maffeo Pantaleoni, the economist, says, "Ten hours at my desk do not tire me at all," and adds that work is to him joy or pain according to the results of his labours, but that "the ardour does not diminish, for it is feverish determination and perseverance. I never feel weary." The Danish philosopher Herald Hoffding says: "I have rarely been able to work for long on a single subject.

"I have to handle various subjects by turns. I can work five hours in the morning and another five in the evening when I am in good form."

The hours of work are to him "perhaps the greatest moments of happiness that life has to offer."

Roberto Ardigo declares, "Work is for me an irresistible need. I work until tired out, but the weariness is accompanied by a sense of satisfaction in the work done." The astronomer Schiapparelli replies that he has nearly always worked ten hours a day, between the ages of twenty-five and sixty, and has even worked sixteen hours consecutively at the same occupation. He further states that to remain idle has always been a torture to him. The writer Arturo Graf, says that he works with great willingness, for to him work is "a source of living joy," but that he finds it very wearisome to have to write even a short article by request and on a given subject.

The artists' replies all agree in asserting that their work brings them such joy as to keep them from feeling weary. The very few answers which speak of incapacity to work for any length of time, or the hardship occasioned by work are accompanied by statements regarding ill-health or other physical handicaps.

It could be argued that the cases mentioned refer to exceptional personalities. The objection would not be valid, however, for we have seen that even these persons are ill-disposed towards occupations which do not absorb or interest them.

The case of Gustave Flaubert is typical from this point of view. He often worked eighteen hours at his desk without pause, but at certain times his work lay heavily on him; when, for instance, he was only putting finishing touches of style, or when engaged in making preparatory investigation.

While he was writing *Madame Bovary* he said in a letter (September 17th, 1835), "I hope that in a month's time the Bovary will have the arsenic in her belly" — which remark is explained by a passage in another letter of the same month (September 20th): "I am working badly, without pleasure, rather with distaste. I am really tired of this work; it is now become a veritable penance to me." When in 1858 he was writing *Salammbo* one chapter of which took him three months of intense work, he wrote to a friend: "Each evening I tumble into bed as worn out as a labourer who has been breaking stones on the highway."

That which is observable in the great personalities is also apparent in the average man. Good results from intellectual work of lengthy duration can be achieved by everyone provided that it is stimulated by "interest," in the spiritual sense of the word. To say "I work without getting tired" means "I work without being conscious of fatigue."

An accountant and an astronomer who both work at calculations — the former at simple and the latter at very complicated — both become tired; but while the former, not being animated by any passion for knowledge, feels the full weight of drudgery, the latter finds vital inspiration in the dry mechanism of his formulae, a light which bids him remain vigilant, keeping him alert and wakeful and masking weariness. The negative element in work is boredom. Boredom is continuous consciousness of tiredness and also at the same time a factor of that tiredness.

The relation between boredom and fatigue is just as valid for manual as for intellectual work, for any physical activity implies of necessity a measure of intellectual effort.

Physical fatigue is more or less intense according to the condition of spirit in which it is carried out. Boredom is a depressive element. It shows as torpor in intellectual work. The person who works with a bored mind is reduced to a state of drowsiness. In manual work boredom lengthens the time.

Michelet, in his memoirs, tells of his experiences, as a boy while working at his father's printing-press: "Immobile in the cashier's desk, under the weight of boredom, nothing but boredom, I learned the meaning of long hours."

How is it possible to keep boredom away from work? That is the problem arising out of these considerations. Work is always tiring. We must endeavour to find out how it may become satisfying tiredness for all.

Every manifestation of energy is accompanied by a feeling of pleasure when it is proportioned to the strength of the organism.

A walk is pleasant, but a forced march is a penance. In the same way, any activity which follows a spontaneous impulse is pleasant. When, on the other hand, an individual is obliged by external conditions to act in opposition to his natural tendencies, he exhausts himself in his effort of will on himself, with consequent suffering and lessened productive capacity.

These considerations lead to the following conclusions:

1. The duration of work must be proportional to the effort involved.
2. Everyone must be free to follow that productive capacity to which they feel most attracted. With regard to the duration of working time, the type of occupation must be taken into account; there are certain essentially uninspiring occupations which thus appear lengthy; it is therefore necessary to consider the time taken from the subjective point of view, that is, taking into account the psychical reflex which the work induces in the person who does it. There are certain jobs which, although "light" because they do not require a large expenditure of muscular energy are nevertheless extremely tiring because uninteresting and as such are the cause of an enormous waste of nervous energies.

The second point is connected with the first. Since any occupation is the more tiring the less interesting it is, it follows that everyone will become less tired, and will therefore work longer and more efficiently, when he is allowed to develop his activity in the field of his own choice.

This is not possible without the economic emancipation and technical development of the worker. When, as Carlyle predicted every individual will be able to choose as his sphere of work that to which he is naturally inclined, work will no longer be labour, and will become a joy for many.

Many lazy people are like that personage in the play *The Hotel of the Poor* who says: "When work is pleasant, life is beautiful. Find me pleasurable work and I will work."

### "Lazy" People and the Problem of Free Work

Many "lazy" people would work could they find an occupation suited to their psychic and physical personality. Kropotkin writes on the subject in *Conquest of Bread*:

> Somebody has said that dust is matter in the wrong place. The same definition applies to nine-tenths of those called lazy. They are people gone astray in a direction that does not answer to their temperament nor to their capacities. In reading the biography of great men, we are struck with the number of "idlers" among them. They were lazy so long as they had not found the right path; afterwards they became labourious to excess. Darwin, Stephenson, and many others belonged to this category of idlers.
>
> Very often the idler is but a man to whom it is repugnant to spend all his life making the eighteenth part of a pin, or the hundredth part of a watch, while he feels he has exuberant energy which he would like to expend elsewhere. Often, too, he is a rebel who cannot submit to being fixed all his life to a work-bench in order to procure a thousand pleasures for his employer, while knowing himself to be far the less stupid of the two, and knowing his only fault to be that of having been born in a hovel instead of coming into the world in a castle.
>
> Lastly, an immense number of "idlers" are idlers because they do not know well enough the trade by which they are compelled to earn their living. Seeing the imperfect thing they make with their own hands, striving vainly to do better, and perceiving that they never will succeed on account of the bad habits of work already acquired, they begin to hate their trade, and, not knowing any other, hate work in general. Thousands of workmen and artists who are failures suffer from this cause.
>
> On the other hand, he who since his youth has learned to play the piano well, to handle the plane *well*, the chisel, the brush, or the file, so that he feels that what he does is *beautiful*, will never give up the piano, the chisel, or the file. He will find pleasure in his work which does not tire him, so long as he is not overdriven.
>
> Under the one name, *idleness*, a series of results due to different causes have been grouped, of which each one could be a source of good, instead of being a source of evil to society.
>
> Like all questions concerning criminality and related to human faculties, facts have been collected having nothing in common with one another. People speak of laziness or crime, without giving themselves the trouble to analyse the cause. They are in a hurry to punish these faults without inquiring if the punishment itself does not contain a premium on "laziness" or "crime."
>
> This is why a free society, if it saw the number of idlers increasing in its midst, would no doubt think of looking first for the cause of laziness, in order to suppress it, before having recourse to punishment. When it is a case, as we have already mentioned, of simple bloodlessness, then before stuffing the brain of a child with science, nourish

his system so as to produce blood, strengthen him, and, that he shall not waste his time, take him to the country or to the seaside; there, teach him in the open air, not in books — geometry, by measuring the distance to a spire, or the height of a tree; natural sciences, while picking flowers and fishing in the sea; physical science while building the boat he will go to fish in. But for mercy's sake do not fill his brain with classical sentences and dead languages. Do not make an idler of him! ...

Or, here is a child which has neither order nor regular habits. Let the children first inculcate order among themselves, and later on, the laboratory, the workshop, the work that will have to be done in a limited space, with many tools about, under the guidance of an intelligent teacher, will teach them method. But do not make disorderly beings out of them by your school, whose only order is the symmetry of its benches, and which — true image of the chaos in its teachings — will never inspire anybody with the love of harmony, of consistency, and method in work.

These reflections by Kropotkin are absolutely right, and given the space I could quote corroborating opinions by psychologists, physicians and teachers, but they do not solve the problem for the immediate future. We can be convinced, as was Zola, that "if all that people were required to do was pleasing work, freely chosen, there would certainly no longer be "lazy people;" we can be convinced that a time will come when no coercion will be necessary to ensure that all shall work; but the problem now for us once the bourgeois regime has fallen is this: is production to be entirely free, that is, entrusted to the population's will to work?

"Attractive work" if universal, presupposes not only free choice and the right to change occupation, compatible with the needs of production, but also the taking over by machines of quite unattractive operations. Kropotkin, when speaking of pleasant work, cites as the subjects of such work the book, the luxury article, the work of art — and not mechanical parts, articles of strict necessity, unpleasantly smelling raw materials, and the like.

Work will become lighter and less dangerous, will cease to be injurious or very tiring, but on the whole it will be slow to become so attractive as to bring about the disappearance of lazy people.

Kropotkin (*Conquest of Bread* 1892) and Grave (*The Dying Society* and *Anarchy* 1894) have not resolved the problem, limiting themselves to a statement that all men who are fit to work should compel themselves to do a certain number of hours work. Many anarchists oscillate between "the right to idleness" and "compulsory work for all," unable to conceive of an intermediate formula, which it seems to me, could be "no compulsion to work, but no duty towards those who do not want to work."

Malatesta wrote in one of his articles, "It seems to me that the reaction to the wishful thinking so prevalent in our circles is an excess of pessimism on the part of others who fail to bear in mind, in this special case of the 'will to work', the moral coercion of public opinion and the immediate effect which a revolution carried out against the exploiters — that is, against those who do not work — is likely to have on men's feelings." But he also wrote, "Basic to the anarchist system, before communism or any other form of social conviviality is the principle of the free compact; the rule of integral communism — 'from each according to his ability, to each according to his need' — applies only to those who accept it, including naturally the conditions which make it practicable."

While recognising the effects of moral coercion, Malatesta does not exclude economic coercion, represented by the sanction which bars "chronic idlers" from communist or collectivist associations. Luigi Fabbri in an article on *The Problem of Free Work* wrote:

> One of the most serious problems that arise when one is considering the practical organisation of a society without governments or masters is that of voluntary work in relation to the necessities of social life. In present-day society, based on struggle and competition, work is in most cases literally a sign of servitude, and for many (especially the manual labourer) inferiority. The majority work because obliged to from need and the fear of starvation, or are impelled to by promises or hopes of a bonus, or a betterment in their conditions which will enable them to leave the exploited class and enter that of the 'privileged'.
>
> What will take the place of the urge of necessity and the desire for profit in a society which ensures to everybody at least the satisfaction of the more elementary needs, in which the spectre of misery and hunger will no longer be a spur, and in which individual remuneration will be replaced by the distribution of goods according to needs, independently of work done?
>
> Up to now, anarchist writers, with one or two exceptions, have sought to eliminate these objections with over-optimistic axiomatic replies which certainly ended the argument; but a close examination showed them to be highly questionable opinions, unsafe predictions, and hopes which presupposed the solution of a number of other very grave problems which still remain.
>
> The opinions, predictions and hopes regarding the solution of this difficult question were not — and are not — mistaken; they all contain, in fact, an indisputable basis of truth and common sense. But they are only partly reasonable and true, or they are so only according to an abstract logic and in relation to future moral and social progress still too far ahead …
>
> One of the dangers of the revolution will actually be the loathing for work which it will inherit from the society of today. We were made aware of this in those brief moments in which it seemed that the revolution was beating at the gates. Too many people among the poor, too many workers really believed that the time had come not to work or to make only the leisured classes work. There were many who did not perceive the obvious truth — that the idle rich were too few in number adequately to take the place of the enormous army of workers and peasants in the fields of

work, and that in any case they would be virtually incapable of giving to society that particular kind of work which would be most needed.

A revolution of people who had no desire to work, or who even only imagined they could rest awhile or work less, would be a revolution condemned to defeat. Under the pressure of necessity, coercive organisms would rapidly form, and these, in the absence of free work, would lead us back to a regime of forced, and, therefore, exploited, labour.

The consciousness of the workers, and particularly revolutionaries and anarchists must, therefore, before the revolution — from this very moment — be awakened to the clear notion that the revolution will mean sacrifice and not merry-making; that during its development not only the armed enemy but also more difficult living conditions will have to be overcome, the latter with harder, longer and more intelligent work. If this work is done voluntarily and in the required measure, well and good — the revolution will triumph. Otherwise that same work will still be done, but this time by compulsion; and that will mean a new coercive, exploiting regime will have reformed on the ruins of the old, and the revolution will have once more failed in attaining its aim.

One of the first things, therefore, that the anarchists must do during the revolution is to organise free and voluntary work. In fact we must make an immediate start in realising this necessity, without worrying whether the revolution is near or far. At the same time we must work to form within the proletariat in general and among the revolutionaries in particular, this idea of the necessity of work, and produce together, with elements to hand in present-day society, and without lulling ourselves into hoping for miracles, those forms of libertarian organisation which will guarantee the production of the necessities of life during and after the revolution. The more forethought that will have been given as to what should be done, the less difficult will it be to carry out in practice.

There will be an anarchist society, not only when the enemies of liberty have been defeated, and the institutions which hinder libertarian accomplishment overthrown, but also when, a sufficient number of individuals (who wish to live and work together anarchically) will be available to further a society of their own which will be economically self-sufficient and strong enough to defend its existence. The existence of individuals who 'wish to live anarchically' presupposes that they have the 'will to work' — otherwise no Anarchy would be possible. When, therefore, the objection of the plague of idleness is raised, we can only consider it — given an existing anarchist society — as follows: 'How will an anarchist society, deprived of the means of coercion, defend itself from those individuals or minorities who neither carry out, nor feel any obligation to work?'

This question has often been answered in the past simply by avoiding it, that is without giving any direct answer. 'There will be no idlers' it was said 'because work is a physical need for both muscles and intellect and everyone will be willing to work when it is no longer a burden or a compulsion imposed by hunger.'

This is partly true. No-one is idle in the absolute sense of the word. But brain and muscles can be quite adequately exercised by work which serves no useful purpose; riding horse-back or reading novels, indulging in the sport of fencing, or writing bad verse … Work, even in anarchy, will therefore have to meet the necessities of production, in order to satisfy all the individual and social needs of life in common; it will have to be organised, that is, according to the demands on production on the part of all, and certainly not merely for the purpose of exercising the muscles and brains of the producers. It may be that in many cases the useful will coincide with the pleasant; where this is not the case, social use must be the prime consideration.

It follows that a 'discipline' of work is necessary. If this discipline is agreed upon and freely accepted, without the need for coercion, by a number of individuals over a wide enough region to constitute a society, this society will be 'anarchic.'

Fabbri has perceived and clearly indicated that it is a duty and not an anachronism for anarchists to examine for themselves this problem of the "discipline of work."

## The Discipline of Work

Nearly all anarchists tend to agree with Mario Rapisardi's warning: "Leave a man to work for as long as he is able and rest as often as he wishes. If discipline is used indiscriminately, man becomes a machine and society a monastery and a prison."

As a general formula this appears more than acceptable to me; but I do not believe that the workshop, however ideal, can be likened, as Kropotkin does, to a library which one enters and leaves as one pleases. The absence of a universally respected working time leads to a waste of motive power, heat and light, in those cases where individual work is not possible as for example, in a metal foundry. It is true that in certain industries (textile, printing, etc.) there is a certain autonomy to avoid a general hold-up in the event of breakdowns and to save the dispersal of power transmission and thus only use as much power as is required for the job in hand. The electric motor has greatly developed mechanical autonomy by placing complicated machines — such as the linotype — at the artisan's disposal, and many public services have been supplanted by perfected systems like the automatic telephone, which greatly reduces the importance of the telephone exchanges.

Considering industrial work as a whole, however, the limits of autonomy are very narrow and are likely to remain so for a long time to come. It should be borne in mind that the burden of a fixed working-time can be greatly lessened by a reduction of the working hours and by travelling facilities to and from work. The choice of work must be subordinated to production requirements but a developed and accurate statistical method will allow many workers to do that for which they are most prepared or for which they have a particular disposition.

At the present time a great many workers are doing work for which they have neither taste nor aptitude.

Free co-operation in industry is not easily accomplished. In the factory of today, the manager is the organiser of the executive (departmental managers, foremen, etc.) and of the division of labour. The operatives work together to the same end, which, however, is not decided by them. This co-operation is nothing more than the direct effect of the capital which employs them simultaneously. The link between their individual functions and their unity as a productive body is outside of themselves, in the capital which needs and unites them. The linking together of their work seems to them, in theory, to be the plan of the capitalists, and the unity of their collective body appears as its authority, as the power of an alien will which subjects their acts to its ends. Insofar as they co-operate, they are merely a particular mode of existence of capital. The productive force which wage-earners manifest in the form of collective work is consequently the productive force of capital.

The problem of the technical hierarchy, too, is a complex one. Managerial abilities are not consistently associated with qualities of a nature that will ensure the nomination of the most able to executive positions, or that will permit the most able to carry out these functions most effectively. Whereas the workshop technician of today is an "official," in the workshop of tomorrow he should be a "teacher," but this change in management will not be easily brought about.

One aspect of the "discipline" of work is that of "rationalisation." The Taylor system has undergone a rapid deterioration under the capitalist regime. Copley, Taylor's biographer, has observed that "everything must be submitted to the workers' good-will, for without this their technical preparation is of no avail … All attempts to turn the new system against the workers would end in disaster."

Many anarchist writers have criticised the pseudo-rationalisation of work, but very few have set the problem in exact terms. We must examine the question of automatism and specialisation if we wish to reconcile the technical necessities of specialisation with the possibility of avoiding the psychic atrophy due to work organised solely from the economic standpoint. Automatism is negative only when it is an end in itself. The operative who for ten years repeats a restricted number of movements, in the end will become an automaton, not because these gestures are automatic, but because the psychic process which determines them is mechanical.

It is the semi-automatic nature of uninteresting work which makes it burdensome and degrading. If I have to translate from the French one hundred pages of a book which does not interest me in the least, I suffer a double penance; that of the weariness of a boring job, and that of being unable to apply my mind to the many things which occur to me because the job in hand requires concentration. But if I have to remove a few hundred postage stamps from a stamp album I may be bored by this silly pastime, but I am also able to occupy my mind with pleasant and interesting thoughts.

It seems clear to me that the really stupefying occupations (when the hours are not excessive) are not the entirely mechanical ones, but rather those that narrow the attention to a monotonous and restricted field, and at the same time require critical attention. Eight hours passed in writing on an absorbing subject are brief; eight hours passed doing a boring job which permits one to indulge in day-dreaming or light conversation are long; but eight hours spent on a piece of work which is boring and at the same time requires active attention are interminable. Book-keepers suffer more, both physically and mentally, than those workers who do entirely mechanical work. The operative who does a completely mechanical job is rather like a woman with her needlework. He can think about something else, chat with his neighbour or hum a tune. This is because his movements are automatic — they are controlled by his subconscious. (A shoe-maker who was subject to epileptic fits would continue to go through the motions of cutting his leather while unconscious.)

When an action becomes mechanical it results in a decrease of mental activity if the mechanisation is circumscribed and to a stimulation if it is renewed and amplified.

Walking is easy, yet it has cost us great efforts to get used to it. Riding a bicycle and walking on a tight-rope require a considerable effort. Though walking becomes in time automatic in action, once we have started moving, keeping one's balance on a bicycle or tightrope always requires a certain amount of concentration. I doubt whether anyone could read Kant, and understand him, while cycling or tight-rope walking.

Automatism, then, only obtains for simple movements. The pianist whose fingers run rapidly over the keyboard does not have to think where to press them, but the musical expression springs from the grafting of "pathos" and the mnemonic attention with automatic movements of arms and hands.

While the poet may, in the haste of expressing through the written word the image of his inspiration, alter his writing to a kind of shorthand, the pianist must be master of the mechanical process, and the more exact he is in his movements, the more complete will be the musical expression and interpretation. The same applies to the draughtsman, the sculptor, and others.

There is, therefore, no automatic work and non-automatic work, but rather, flatly mechanical work on the one hand and intelligently automatic work on the other. The first is soul destroying if it becomes an end in itself and is done to excess; but within the limits of a time-table proportionate to the individual's physical capacity it is neither damaging nor tedious.

The problem does not lie in avoiding automatism which is more and more required by the development of mechanical industrialism, but rather in alternating work with rest. The master-class, too, has understood this. The paper *Opinion* of September 12th, 1924, published the following: "Careful observation carried out in a number of English factories has shown that, even in jobs where the required muscular energy is of the smallest, the employers obtain an increase in production by allowing rest-periods to their employees.

For example, in the case of a group of women engaged in labelling packages, the introduction of ten-minute rests at regular intervals led to a 13% increase in output in spite of the 2% reduction in the working day.

The same results have been observed in a group of women engaged in assembling bicycle-chains. It should be noted that these rest-periods do not produce the desired results unless they have taken place at specific times as for the work itself.

Production does not increase in the same proportion if work is suspended according to an individual's whim." The discipline of rest is therefore as necessary as the discipline of work. "Discipline of work" means rational distribution of jobs; rational alternation of effort and rest; rational employment of the particular worker's instincts, feelings and mental aptitude; association of the productive process as a whole with the autonomy of the individual: and so on.

## Conclusion

For centuries, everywhere, work has been, and still is, a penance. It is significant that in all Aryan languages those words which indicate a productive effort mean suffering. Man has always worked from necessity, but at the same time there is inherent in man the instinct to work — which is perhaps nothing more than a manifestation of the erotic instinct.

The laziness of certain primitive peoples is not so much stupid indolence as a refusal to adapt themselves to new labours requiring continued attention and generating boredom. Hunting, fishing and stock-breeding are activities somewhere between work and play, and it was mainly economic need, and coercion on the part of conquering warriors, which forced people who lived by hunting and fishing to change to agricultural and then industrial communities. Where the natural conditions required very great effort, while at the same time offering possibilities of land or sea commerce, the people were pre-eminently traders and travellers (Phoenicians, Hebrews, etc.).

Man is "homo faber" inasmuch as he is a political animal, and Ribot rightly says that the love of work "is a secondary sentiment which progresses in step with civilisation."

Love for work, an important conditioning factor of economic and psychic well-being is determined by progress which cannot only be gauged by the "amount" produced, but rather by the idea that work ceases to be drudgery and comes nearer to being a game.

Already under capitalism industrial work is being made more attractive. In a report approved by the Manufacturing Association Congress of Illinois in July, 1931, the stimulating effect of music was praised. Many factories have "rational" lighting, and more attention is being paid to the psycho-physiological influence of colours, sounds, smells, etc.

But all these modernistic notions are vitiated by the intent to exploit. Means and methods are studied whereby the worker shall not be "uselessly" exhausted, in order to make more thorough use of him, and certain enthusiasms for workshop and factory "music while you work" recall, not so much Fourier's sensual, affective and volitional stimuli, as the empirical and utilitarian physiologism of certain wagon-drivers who in order to stimulate their exhausted horses up a steep slope will walk a young mare in front of them.

However, the technique for the emancipation of work within the sphere of production is being perfected, and is paving the way for the time when even in industrial work, man's occupation will be pleasurable. And the day will come when with the machine as the friend of man, everyone will be occupied according to his or her particular preferences, and doing pleasant work. Then their pleasure will spring from their work "like the coloured petals of a life-giving flower." This image of Ruskin's is a bright reflection of the whole of his philosophy as a socialist-humanist writer; but those who search in the writings and speeches of writers and artists of the nineteenth century would find not a few equally eloquent endorsements of Fourier's idea of "attractive work."

D' Annunzio took as his own the motto of the times of the communes: "Effort without weariness" an admirably concise and clear saying, for effort is a law of work, however attractive it may be. The Italian poet has only vaguely guessed the social truth of this motto and only superficially felt its intrinsic moral beauty.

"Effort without weariness" means free work, work in which the personality is uplifted and perfected. How it may move from wishful thinking to historical fact is the problem to be discussed — and we anarchists are the most suited for such an examination; for in the producer we see, first and foremost, a human being; for the cold formulae of the production statisticians are not enough for us — they fail to see what immense treasures are hidden in the deviated and dissipated energies of those who perform the daily drudgery without intellectual light or pleasant feelings, atrophying the wings of their personality and transforming them, in the course of a few years, into ever less human machines.

# THE ART OF SHOVELLING

*Ifan Edwards*

*Extracts from Chapter 10, Manure Works, from No Gold on my Shovel — An Autobiography (The Porcupine Press, London 1947). The author was born in 1898 at Barry Dock. His experiences as a labourer took place in 1919-20, following years in the Army, which he had joined at the age of 16, including two years on the Western Front.*

I took the place of another man who had been sent to do some job or other in the opposite end of the mill. My partner in shovelling was again a smallish man, competent with a shovel but not a very energetic worker, so that my lack of experience did not show up a great deal.

I had never been used to a shovel, and like all others who have not earned their livings with one I imagined there was nothing to it. It looked so easy to thrust into the pile and lift up a heap of stuff, step backwards with one foot and throw the load neatly over the left shoulder as you straightened up.

I kept a surreptitious eye on my partner and did exactly as he did, but after three fillings of the skip I was pouring with perspiration in trying to keep pace with his easy, rhythmical movements. We were not on piecework, but the big hopper up in the roof was running dangerously low and the foreman wanted it full. Three skips running in turn could fill it faster than the mills could eat it up, but the defection of one supply-line made all the difference and meant that we had to go all out to keep the mills going.

By teatime I was feeling it badly; my back was cracking with the constant bending up and down and my hands were fearfully sore. I sat down on the plank resting on a few bricks which comprised the messroom, and leaned back gratefully against the cool whitewashed wall to eat and drink. There was an open brazier on the floor upon which we could warm our tea-jacks, and for twenty minutes we luxuriated before getting stiffly to our feet again.

Four more hours to go. They were four of the longest hours I had ever known. I shovelled mechanically, piling up the skip and pushing it along the rails to the hoist, tipping it and running it back empty under its own momentum while we followed wearily after. Then down to it again, bending and lifting, settling the load on the big number seven square-faced shovels and heaving it into the skip at our backs. It was a warm evening, and we pulled off our shirts and worked stripped to the waist to keep cool.

The dust settled on our skins and worked its way into the open pores as we perspired, and when the end of the shift came we looked pretty sights. There was no thought of washing, and we just shook some of the dust out of our clothes and thankfully went home.

The next morning found me in such a state that I really did not think I could do another shift. When I had arrived home the previous night I had been actually unable to turn the door-handle because of the agonising blisters on my hands, and I had had to kick the door gently for the landlady to come and open it. I tried to wash, but the dust was engrained in the skin and refused to come off unless a nailbrush were used, and you can't use a nailbrush on soft blisters. The backs of my hands where they had rubbed against my knees in shovelling were deprived of skin, and from head to foot I was one throbbing ache.

I thought hard as to what I should do, looking doubtfully at my hands as I tried to open and shut them. If I jibbed at any more punishment, I should be out of a job again; maybe the pain would wear off in a few days. But my hands worried me. I could not hold a knife or fork firmly, let alone a shovel; and to close my fists was agony. I deferred a decision until after dinner, as I would not be leaving for work until about half past one.

I was still undecided at one o'clock, but I had dressed in my dusty working clothes, buckled on my belt, and left my boots unlaced because I could not do them up. I tried my hands again, opening and shutting them, and they felt a little better. I got up, picked up my food-box, and set off to work.

The long walk down to the works eased the stiffness from my legs, and altogether I had nearly recovered my spirits by the time I got into the mill. There was the skip again, and the two shovels lying on the floor where the morning shift had left them, and my mate of yesterday cleaning loose bits from under his feet ready for a start. Neither of us had shaved. I took off my coat, rolled up my sleeves, and caught hold of the shovel. There was only one way to go about it, and that was to grip loosely with my fingertips until such time as my hands should warm up and fold properly round the thick handle with its steel strappings, and with many wincings as my sore body protested against movement I bent down and drove into the heap.

Four hours afterwards I was all right. I was glad I had stuck it. My hands were burning, but not too painfully, and I had worked off the excruciating pain in the small of my back. By dint of careful imitation of the methods of my partner I got into the rhythm of the throw, and made up for my still obvious lack of skill by lifting much more than he did with the shovel.

I had a lot to learn about this business, but towards the end of the shift I was conceited enough to think that I had mastered the job. How far I was from being anywhere near mastery I was yet to discover, because the technique of the shovel, if one is to be a real artist with it, demands long practice. A navvy, using his shield-shaped excavating shovel in a trench with a bad bottom, does wonders, but in a long time; he would be a useless partner in a ten-ton wagon, and the corporation employee, lifting little bits in the street, would have died of fright had he seen our shovels.

Having broken myself in, I was now keen to become an artist in shovelry, and slogged away until my mate was forced to protest that we were not on piecework.

We "spelled up," the hopper was decently full, the nightshift were coming in, and I had earned another nine shillings ...

The next shift to be worked was nights, ten o'clock at night till six in the morning, a new experience for me. I rather liked the novelty of it. My mate didn't show up, and I heard that he had packed up and left. He was a bird of passage who hadn't stayed there more than a week or so, and I was beginning to feel quite an old hand.

The foreman knew me now, and became quite friendly as he introduced me to a new partner, a short, wiry chap whose last job had been underground, and I asked him why he had left. An accident, he said; a fall of roof in his working-place had pinned him under a great stone, which he had supported with his body for many hours before he was rescued.

I was not surprised at this, because when stripped he showed a magnificently muscled torso with wide shoulders and rather longish arms, and when later those arms wore boxing-gloves at their extremities he had one of the wickedest and most far-reaching lefts I had ever failed to dodge. He didn't feel it necessary to tell me that while he had been braced under that stone his left hand had been crushed by another one, so that now the shattered bones of his left thumb-joint were secured at base by gold wire, and his mining days were over. It did not affect his grip to any great extent, though, in which he was lucky, for he was a man whose skill with a shovel was little short of the marvellous.

Patsy and I started that night a partnership which lasted twelve months. He was left-handed, thus making himself the perfect counterthrow to my right-handed orthodoxy, and no-one will ever see his like with a shovel again. He was its master; it was part of him. He could use it with equal and tireless facility on either "hand," an accomplishment seldom met with in the ranks of the manual labourers, and he was a fierce and determined worker, prepared to keep pace with any two ordinary men for so long as they liked.

He watched me at work for a few minutes, and then showed me how it should be done. I was shovelling with my arms only, which was hard work; I wasn't using my legs to drive it, and I was holding it too stiffly. "You'll kill yourself like that," said Patsy. "Try it this way," and he slung the blade of the shovel towards the heap until it touched the edge, then followed up with both knees driving hard against the back of his hands to supply the power.

A quick downward jerk of the wrist loaded the shovel, it was withdrawn slightly; swung backwards as the body straightened, then delivered over the shoulder into the skip with a graceful sway and twist of the trunk, so that the whole body handled the weight with the utmost economy of effort. The shovel and its motion seemed but an extension of those long arms; there was a clean swift controlled grace about his movements which was a delight to watch.

I waited to time myself with him and chimed in with his powerful strokes; drive, jerk, swing back, up and over, all in one cycle of motion which made shovelling an art to be studied and not merely a distasteful task for the unskilled.

We had filled three or four skips when he paused and said, "That's the way, man. You've got it now." I had never felt more pleased. Here was another branch of the labouring arts well on the way to being mastered, and I was being taught by an expert. Our skip was now the first to be filled; Patsy saw to that, and we placed our shovel-blades upside-down against the heap to make seats and had a spell while the other two pairs loaded theirs, and we would then take it in turn to run the skip to the lift.

There was quite a knack in starting off the full skip with its ton and a quarter weight, a knack which Pats (as he was usually called) had learned underground with coal trams; a steady heave with the back and legs braced against a steel sleeper in the track. The interval of waiting for the others steadily lengthened, and became long enough for Pats to think of tipping one of the wagons on the ramp above us as a spare-time job in between skips. There was a good chance of our being able to do this because the hopper over the mill was now practically full and the other men could afford to take it easy.

They, however, took the opportunity of resting on the plank seat when they had a chance, as they had slogged hard to help fill the hopper and were entitled to a rest. Pats didn't want a rest; he wanted wagons, which would increase our earnings for the shift by three shillings shared between us. It meant throwing out ten tons of the stuff direct to the floor, occasionally filling a skip with it if the hopper were suffering from inattention.

I didn't feel much like taking on a wagon that night, though, so we decided to let things stand until the next shift and take things easy for the rest of the night. We had a nice long interval for "supper" and restarted at about two o'clock in the morning, feeling full of beans because we had the job licked and the hopper would be brimming over. In about an hour we were leaning back on our wooden seat near the brazier and trying to talk above the roar of the machinery at our backs …

During those first few weeks in the mill I did nothing else but develop my technique with the shovel. I learned to throw on the other hand like Pats did, which avoided the awkward business of throwing "cross-handed" when your partner couldn't take the opposite hand, and we got to know each other's methods so well that we changed hands by instinct when circumstances demanded it.

And as for the full wagons on the ramp on our side, we used to come in to work hoping that the previous shift had been too lazy to empty them, for there were usually three of these wagons pushed in daily on either side of the mill. There was nothing more certain than that Patsy would collar the three on our side if he could; it meant nine shillings between us, although it also meant throwing thirty tons over and above our normal tonnage for the shift, and every pound of it had to be flung from our shovels.

But Patsy went about things most scientifically, as he did about the shovelling and his boxing. The wagons had drop-sides, so we would knock out the release-pins of the doors and allow a good deal to fall out before we climbed up into them.

Then Pats would clear a foothold on one side, and I on the other, and work into the stuff until we met in the centre, where we would drive a pathway through the middle of the truck, a yard wide. Then the fun would start. Off would come our shirts, and we would sweep the stuff out, not shovel it, with a motion like that of a man with a scythe, our shovels driving great heaps before them in swift flashing strokes which made the pile literally vanish under our hands while sometimes the foreman would stand watching, rubbing his chin while two apparently half-naked lunatics tore into his wagons.

Ten tons in 20 minutes was our record on this job; we timed ourselves once when we were very fresh at the beginning of a shift, and Patsy was always one to try something to break a record.

So we worked in unison, becoming fast friends with the most implicit trust in each other. We were proud of being the fastest skip in the mill, and I was very proud to have such a mate. Once stripped, gripping his shovel, he was a joy to watch. He was not very big, but he had the strength of a lion allied to a sweep of shoulder astonishing in its breadth and power.

Silky bunches of muscle cased his whole torso; he was perfectly developed, and he made the hard manual labour serve as training for the feats of strength he was constantly trying. He astonished the boys at the bagging-off end one night by picking up two of their fifty-six-pound [25 *kilograms* – ed] weights and drilling with them as one does with dumb-bells, and on another occasion he stood over a fallen two-hundred-weight [102kg] bag of manure and lifted it clean from the floor to his shoulder and walked off with it to the wagons. Small as he was, he was afraid of no one, and the local boxing fraternity soon entertained a healthy respect for him. My own feelings towards him were compounded, I think, of warm admiration with a touch of envy.

As time wore on we worked in friendly rivalry with the four other fellows running the skips, persuading them to go all out with us at the beginning of the shifts to fill the hopper and ensure a nice long spell towards the end of the turn, and after some weeks we were more or less a well-knit and established team of skipmen who could be guaranteed to do their whack and a good deal more if it were necessary.

This novel accession to his strength removed the foreman altogether from our end of the mill; he had nothing to worry about, and unlike most foremen did not find us another job after we had slogged hard to earn a rest. We discovered that he was a most good-hearted fellow, who previous to our coming had gone through a very bad time with the labourers at the skip end and was now very pleased to find a gang who were really interested in keeping things going without having to be driven to it.

The only time he ever became a bit regimental was on the morning shift, six till two, round about nine o'clock when the manager and his staff were due to arrive, but, knowing the reason, we didn't take any notice of an occasional admonishment for taking too long over our breakfasts.

These breakfasts were amusing feasts, with bacon cooked in the hollow of our shovels over the open brazier. It probably sounds a filthy process, but no frying-pan was ever more thoroughly scoured than were our shovel-blades, and a wipe with a piece of clean waste removed the dust from the hollows, it having the additional advantage of enabling us to sit four feet away from the fire and still do the cooking. The tea-cans of those who brought their drink ready-made stood around the foot of the brazier, and those who made tea on the spot threw the leaves into their cans of boiling water on top of the fire. Each to his choice.

The Goblin of The Coal Bin

This censorious Olean Evening Times cartoon attacking striking US miners was published in October 1919, around the same time as Edwards was learning his new job on the other side of the Atlantic.

Alongside a 60% increase in pay, the rebellious bituminous coal miners were demanding a six-hour day and a five-day week. The 1919 strike would herald the start of a three-year campaign involving 400,000 workers.

# MEASURING MISERY

### John Hewetson

*John Hewetson (1913-1990) was a member of the Freedom Press group and an editorial writer for Freedom newspaper from 1940-54. With other editors of Freedom he was given a nine-month prison sentence for sedition in 1945 in what became a celebrated free speech case. He and his co-defendants' right to tell soldiers to use their arms to defend liberty after the war, rather than just the British State, was backed by famous names including George Orwell and Herbert Read. The British Medical Journal (Vol. 285) in its Personal Paper series published a short account by Hewetson of his three prison terms. He authored Freedom Press publications including Ill-Health Poverty and the State (1946), Sexual Freedom for the Young (1951) and Mutual Aid and Social Evolution (1946). This essay first appeared in Freedom in 1954.*

In the past the movements for social reform have had fairly concrete conditions to fight against: gross poverty, gross illiteracy, high mortality from disease and child-bearing. All of them easy to demonstrate and relatively easy to measure. The Welfare State can therefore point to considerable triumphs in the reduction of these ills, and all too often social reformers look at the figures and express a satisfaction that is smug in that it does not look for fresh fields to conquer.

But if one looks at life today one cannot but sense the unhappiness and frustration which welfare measures simply do not touch. Human happiness and contentment involve so much more than improved material conditions, housing, educational facilities and the like stock in trade of the reformer. To say this is not to decry the importance of material alleviations, only to insist that they do not by themselves produce the good life.

But these very phrases — unhappiness, frustration, contentment, the good life — all illustrate the difficulties of those who want more than family allowances and council flats — the difficulty of measuring such concepts. A similar difficulty existed in the thirties when the campaign against malnutrition began in earnest. What constituted malnutrition? While the argument centred round failure or success in achieving such and such a diet, little progress was made.

But when Sir John Boyd Orr (now Lord Boyd Orr) insisted that starvation was to be measured not against *minimum* diets but against an *optimum* one progress began to be made very rapidly indeed. Orr urged that the only proper standard of measurement was a diet such that no additions to it could effect an improvement in health. And he found that such a diet was enjoyed by only about 20% of the population.

This realisation gave more impetus to the improvement of nutrition than it had ever received before and many manifestations of malnutrition common in the '30s are now scarcely ever seen.

The problem of human unhappiness remains a much more difficult one to measure and therefore to bring home to the statistics-loving reformers of our time. But an investigation by a group of family doctors widely reported in the popular press this week does make a start in this direction. Doctors engaged in urban, suburban and rural practices came together to provide an answer to the question: how much of the illness they treat is due to stress and distress as against organic disease? The account of their investigations (published on February 1st in the *Practitioner*) opens with the unemphatic remark: "That much illness in Britain in the present day reflects mental unrest no one can doubt." Their conclusion is stated equally soberly:

"By and large these figures show that about one fifth of the patients seen (for the first time) on any one day in an urban practice suffer from stress disorders; in the country, the proportion will be 10-15% ... The figures for the town and suburban practices in spring and summer show that almost half of those patients who return for further treatment and advice have an illness associated with emotional tension."

These percentages reveal at a stroke the enormous amount of unhappiness and strain to which people are subjected in one of the most advanced and stable countries in the world. For it must be remembered that these doctors were measuring the proportion of patients whose stress and distress caused them to seek medical relief: there must be many more whose unhappiness did not reflect itself in functional illness, or whose own awareness told them the nature of their trouble without their going to the doctor.

The stress illnesses are the result of life situations which do not make for happiness and their study reveals a thousand ways in which present day life frustrates human beings. To recognise the extent of this daily defeat of happiness should be the starting point of an attempt to make the human environment in line with life aspirations. But to set one's hand to this task requires the willingness to see the human situation whole and to range oneself whole-heartedly on the side of life-enhancing forces.

Such concepts require the abandonment of the niggling methods of statistics and percentages and measurement, in favour of warmth and sympathy, solidarity and wisdom.

# THE WAGE SYSTEM

*Peter Kropotkin*

*Vernon Richards' 1983 translation of The* Wage System/Le Salariat *was written using the* Temps Nouveaux *(Paris) edition of 1911, though the essay was first published in* La Revolte *in 1888 and translated for* Freedom *newspaper in 1889. Scans of the original can be found, along with all* Le Revolte's *back issues from 1887-1894, at archivesautonomies.org.*

In their plans for the reconstruction of society, the collectivists commit, in our opinion, a twofold error. While speaking of abolishing the capitalist regime, they would wish, nevertheless, to maintain two institutions on which the regime depends: representative government and the wage system.

As regards so called representative government, we have often spoken about it. It is quite beyond our comprehension how intelligent people — and the collectivist party does not lack such people — can continue to be supporters of national or municipal parliaments, after all the lessons we have learned from history, in England and Germany as well as in Switzerland and the United States. While on all sides we witness the collapse of the parliamentary regime, and while on all sides there is a growing criticism of *the very principles* of the system — no longer just of their application — how is it that intelligent people calling themselves socialist-revolutionaries try to maintain a system already condemned to disappear?

One knows that the system was developed by the bourgeoisie in order to confront the monarchy and at the same time to maintain and increase its power over the workers. This is the typical method of procedure of bourgeois rule. One knows that in advocating it the middle classes have never seriously maintained that a parliament or a municipal council represents either the nation or the city; the more intelligent among them know that that is impossible. In supporting the parliamentary system, the bourgeoisie has simply tried to stem the power of the monarchy without giving liberty to the people.

Furthermore, one realises that as people become more aware of their interests and as the variety of interests increases, the system can no longer function. And consequently the democrats in every country seek, without success, all kinds of palliatives, and correctives to the system.

The *referendum* is tried out and is found to be worthless; there is talk of proportional representation, of representation for minorities — all mere parliamentary utopias. In a word the utmost is done to find what cannot be found: that is a body of delegates to represent millions of different interests in the nation; but one is obliged to recognise that one is taking the wrong road and then confidence in a government by delegation vanishes.

Only the socialist-democrats and the collectivists do not lose this confidence and seek to maintain the so called national representation, and it is this that we just cannot understand.

If our anarchist principles do not suit them, if they find them inapplicable, at least they should, it seems to us, try to predict what other system of organisation would square with a society without capitalists and landowners. But to take the system of the bourgeois — a system which is dying, a vicious system if ever there was one — and to commend it with a few minor amendments, such as the imperative mandate, or the referendum, the uselessness of which has already been demonstrated, and to advocate it for a society which will have undergone a social revolution — we find this incomprehensible, unless one is using the term social revolution but advocating anything but revolution, that is a trivial patching up of the existing bourgeois regime.

The same can be said for the wage system; for after having proclaimed the abolition of private property and the possession in common, of the instruments of production, how can one advocate the continuation of the wage system in one form or another, yet, this is just what the collectivists are doing when they recommend labour tokens to us. If the English socialists at the beginning of the nineteenth century proposed labour tokens, one could understand it. They were simply seeking to reconcile capital and labour. They rejected any idea of violently laying hands on the property of capitalists. They were so far from being revolutionary that they declared a willingness to submit themselves even to the imperial regime, so long as that regime favoured their cooperative societies. Deep down they remained bourgeois, charitable, if you like, and it is for this reason — Engels tells us why in the preface to the *Communist Manifesto* of 1848 — that at that time *socialists* were members of the bourgeoisie whereas progressive workers were *communists*.

If at a later date Proudhon took up this idea again, this too can be understood. In his mutualist system what was he seeking if not to render capital less objectionable, even though it involved the maintenance of individual property, which he detested from the bottom of his heart, but which he thought necessary as a guarantee for the individual against the State ...

That economists who are more or less bourgeois should also accept labour tokens this too can be understood. It is of no importance to them whether workers are paid in labour tokens or in coins minted with the effigy of the Republic or the Empire. In the coming debacle they are concerned to save private ownership of occupied houses, the land, factories, or at least of occupied houses and the capital needed for the manufacturing industry. And in order to maintain that property, labour tokens would answer their purpose very well.

So long as the labour token can be exchanged for jewellery and carriages, the landlord will gladly accept them as payment for rent. And so long as the occupied house, the field and the factory belong to the bourgeois it will be necessary to pay these bourgeois in some way or other to persuade them to allow you to work in their fields or in their factories and to lodge in their houses. It will be necessary to pay a wage to the worker, to pay him for his work either in gold, or in paper money, or in labour tokens that can be exchanged for all kinds of commodities.

But how can one advocate that new form of wage — the labour token — if one grants that the house, the field and the factory are no longer private property; that they belong to the commune or to the nation.

## Work and pay

Let us look more closely at this system of payment for work done advocated by the French, German, English and Italian collectivists.*

It boils down to the following, more or less: Everybody works, either in the fields, in factories, in schools, hospitals and so on. The working day is determined by the State, to which everything, from the land, factories to the means of communication, belong. Each worker having done a day's work receives a labour token, which is marked let's. say "Eight hours work." With this token, he can obtain from the State warehouses, or from the different corporations all kinds of goods. The token can be split up so that one can purchase an hour's worth of meat, ten minute's worth of matches, or half an hour's worth of tobacco. Instead of saying: four penn'orth of soap, after the collectivist revolution one will ask for five minutes worth of soap.

Most collectivists, loyal to the distinction established by the bourgeois economists (and by Marx too) between skilled work and unskilled work, tell us that skilled or professional work will have to be paid at a higher rate than unskilled work. Thus an hour's work by a doctor will have to be considered as equal to two or three hours work by a nurse or to three hours work by a labourer.

"Professional or skilled work will be a multiple of unskilled labour" declares the collectivist Groenland, because that kind of work requires a longer or shorter apprenticeship. Other collectivists, such as the French Marxists, do not make this distinction. They proclaim "the equality of wages." The doctor, the school teacher and the professor will be paid with labour tokens at the same rate as the labourer. Eight hours spent doing the rounds of the hospital wards will be worth as much as eight hours spent on navvying, or in the mines or in the factories.

---

*\* The Spanish anarchists, in retaining the term collectivists, understand by this word the common ownership of the instruments of labour and "the freedom of each group to distribute the products of their common efforts in whatever manner they wish," following communistic principles or in quite other ways.*

Some make yet another concession; they admit that unpleasant or unhealthy work — such as work in the sewers — will possibly be paid at a higher rate than pleasant work. An hour's work in the sewers will be reckoned, so they maintain, as two hours work by the professor.

Let us add that some collectivists accept lump payments to corporations. Thus a corporation would say: "Here are 100 tons of steel. To produce it there were 100 of us workers and it took us ten days to produce. Our day being of 8 hours that makes 8,000 hours of work for 100 tons of steel: that is 80 hours per ton," whereupon the State would pay them 8,000 work tokens of one hour each which would then be allocated among the members of the factory, in whatever manner they saw fit.

On the other hand, if a hundred miners took twenty days to extract 8,000 tons of coal, then the coal would be worth two hours a ton, and the 16,000 tokens each worth one hour, received by the miners' corporation would be shared out among themselves according to their own assessment.

In the event of disagreement — if the miners protested and declared that the ton of steel should not cost more than 60 hours labour instead of 80; if the professor wanted to be paid twice as much as the nurse for his day's work — then the State would intervene and settle their differences.

Such is, in a few words, the kind of organisation the collectivists wish to see emerge out of the social revolution. As can be seen their principles are: collective property of the instruments of production, and payment to each according to the number of productive hours, taking into account the productivity of his labour. As to the political regime, it would be the parliamentary system improved by the replacement of the men in power, the imperative mandate and the referendum that is, the yes or no plebiscite on questions which would be submitted to the popular vote.

Let us point out right away that in our opinion this system is completely unworkable.

Collectivists start by proclaiming a revolutionary principle — the abolition of private property — and no sooner have they proclaimed it than they reject it by supporting an organisation of production and consumption that stems from private property.

They proclaim a revolutionary principle and — with an unbelievable lapse of memory seem to be unaware of the consequences that would stem from a principle so different from the existing one. They forget that the very fact of abolishing individual ownership of the instruments of production (land, factories, means of communication, money) must launch society into completely new directions; that it must change production from top to bottom, both in means and ends: that all the day-to-day relations between people must be modified as soon as the land, machines and everything else are looked upon as communal possessions.

They say: "No private property" and forthwith they hasten to uphold private property in its current manifestations.

"For production you will be a community. The fields, the tools, and machines will, they say, be held by you in common. What has been created up to now — those manufactures, those railways, those ports, those mines — will belong to everybody. No distinction whatsoever will be made as to the part played by each of you in the past for producing those machines, for sinking those mines or for building those railways.

"But as from tomorrow, you will argue in great detail among yourselves as to what your share will be to produce more machines, to sink more mines.

"As from tomorrow you will seek to assess exactly what each individual's share will be in the new production. You will count the minutes you work and you will be on the look-out to make sure that a minute's work of your neighbour cannot purchase more than yours.

"You will calculate your hours and minutes at work and since the hour measures nothing, since in any particular manufacture one worker can supervise four trades at once, whereas in another it might be only two — you will have to take into account the muscular energy, the cerebral energy and the nervous energy expended. You will calculate in detail the years of apprenticeship in order to assess exactly each individual's share in future production." All this after having declared that you are taking no account of the part he played in the past.

Well, for us it is obvious that if a nation or a commune gave itself such an organisation it wouldn't last a month. A society cannot organise itself on two absolutely contrary principles — two principles which contradict each other at every step. And the nation or the commune which gave itself such an organisation would be obliged either to return to private property or to transform itself immediately into a communist society.

## On Hierarchies

We have pointed out that most collectivist writers expect that in the socialist society, remuneration will be made by a distinction between skilled or professional work and unskilled work. They maintain that an hour's work by an engineer or an architect must be reckoned to be worth two or three hours' work by the blacksmith, the mason or the nurse. And the same distinction must be made, they say, between workers whose craft demands a more or less prolonged apprenticeship, and those who are only simple labourers.

This is how it happens in bourgeois society; it should also apply to the collectivist society.

Well, to establish this distinction means laying down in advance a line of demarcation between the worker and those who presume to govern him. It is to divide as always society into two quite distinct classes: the aristocracy of knowledge over the plebeian with the horny hands; the one dedicated to the service of the other; the one doing physical work to feed and clothe the other whilst the latter take advantage of their leisure to learn to dominate those who feed them. It is more than that; it is to take one of the distinctive traits of bourgeois society and give it the approval of the social revolution. It is to establish a principle out of an evil custom now condemned in the old society which is on its way out.

We know what reply we shall get. We shall be told about "scientific socialism." The bourgeois economists — and Marx too — will be quoted to us to prove that the scale of wages has its raison d'être, since the "labour power" of the engineer will have cost society more than the "labour power" of the labourer. To be sure! That was necessary, once one had assumed the thankless task of proving that goods are exchanged in proportion to the amount of socially necessary work needed for their production. Without that, Ricardo's theory of value, taken up by Marx in his turn, could not be sustained.

But we also know what to believe on these questions. We know that if the engineer, the academic and the doctor are today paid ten times as much as the worker, it is not because of the "production costs" of these gentlemen. It is because of an educational monopoly.

The engineer, academic, and doctor are simply exploiting a capital asset — their diplomas — just as the bourgeois exploits his factory, or the nobleman exploited his title. The university degree has replaced the birth certificate of the nobleman of the ancien regime. As to the employer who pays the engineer twenty times more than the labourer, he makes the following simple reckoning: if the engineer can save him a hundred thousand francs a year on his production costs, he will pay the engineer twenty thousand. And when he sees a foreman, able to drive the workers and save ten thousand francs in wages, he loses no time in offering him two or three thousand francs a year. He parts with a thousand francs where he counts on gaining ten thousand, and this in essence is the capitalist system.

So let no one come up with this talk about production costs of the labour force, and tell us that a student who has cheerfully spent his youth at a university has a "right" to a salary ten times that of a miner's son who has been wasting away down a mine from the age of eleven. One might as well say that a merchant who has done a twenty years "apprenticeship" in a business house is entitled to draw his hundred francs a day and only pay five to each of his workers.

No-one has ever worked out the production costs of the labour force. And if an idler costs society a lot more than an honest worker, it still remains to be seen when all things are taken into account — mortality among workers' children, the ravages of anaemia, and premature deaths — whether a robust day labourer does not cost society more than an artisan.

Would they have us believe, for example, that the wage of thirty sous that a female worker in Paris receives, or the six sous paid to the peasant woman of the Auvergne to ruin her eyesight at lace- making, represent the "production costs" of these women? We are fully aware of the fact that often they work for even less than that, but we also know that they do so only because, thanks to our wonderful organisation, they would die of hunger without those absurdly low wages.

In today's society, when we see a Ferry or a Floquet paying themselves a hundred thousand francs a year while the worker has to be satisfied with a thousand or less; when we see that the foreman is paid two or three times as much as the worker and that even among the workers themselves, there are all kinds of grades, from 10 francs a day down to the 6 sous of the peasant woman — we are disgusted.

We condemn these differentials. Not only do we disapprove of the high salaries of the Minister, but we also disapprove of the differences between the 10 francs and the 6 sous. It disgusts us just as much. We consider it as unjust and we say: down with privileges in education as well as privileges of birth! Some of us are anarchists, others are socialists, precisely because such privileges disgust us.

But how could we establish privileges in principle? How to proclaim that the privileges of education shall be the basis of an egalitarian society, without delivering a mortal blow at that very society? What has been undergone hitherto, can no longer be accepted in a society based on equality. The general next to the private, the rich engineer next to the worker, the doctor next to the nurse, already, now, fills us with disgust. Could we accept this in a society which sets out to proclaim equality?

Obviously not. Popular conscience, inspired by an egalitarian puff of wind would rebel against such injustice; it would not tolerate it. It were better not to try.

It is for this reason that some French collectivists, having understood how impossible it would be to maintain a scale of wages in a society inspired by the wind of revolution, are now at pains to propose the equality of wages. But in this they come up against other quite as important difficulties, and their equality of wages becomes a utopia as unrealistic as the other's scale of wages.

A society which will have taken possession of all social wealth and loudly proclaimed that "all" have a right to that wealth — whatever part they may have played in the past in creating it — will be obliged to abandon any ideas about wages either in coin or in labour tokens.

## No Accurate Measurements

The collectivists say "To each according to his deeds," or rather according to his share of services rendered to society. And they recommend this principle as the basis for society once the revolution will have made available to all the instruments of labour and all that is needed for production!

Well, if the social revolution had the misfortune to declare that principle, it would arrest the development of mankind for a whole century; it would be a case of building on sand; it would, in fact be leaving unsolved the whole vast social problem that we have inherited from past centuries.

Indeed, in a society such as ours, where we can see that the harder a man works the less is he paid, that principle may appear at first sight as an aspiration towards justice. But in reality it is but the ratification of all existing injustices. It is by that principle that the wage system started, to end where it is today, in flagrant inequalities and all the abomination of contemporary society. And it has ended in this way because from the moment society began to value services rendered in money terms or in every kind of wage — from the day when it was declared that everyone would receive only that which he succeeded in being paid for his efforts — the whole history of capitalist society (with the aid of the State) was written in advance; it was contained, in embryo, in this principle.

Must we then return to the point of departure and go over the same ground all over again? Our theoreticians want to; but fortunately that is impossible: we have said that the revolution will be communistic; if it is not it will be drowned in blood.

Services rendered to society — be it work in the factory or in the fields, or social services — *cannot* be reckoned in money terms. There can be no accurate measurement of value: neither of what has been wrongly called practical exchange value nor of usage value. If we see two people both working five hours a day for the community over a period of years on two different jobs which equally please them, we can say that, on the whole, their labours are equivalent.

But one cannot break up their work, and say that the product of each day's or hour's or minute's work by one man equals the product of each hour or minute of the other worker. For us the present wage scale is a complex product of taxes, government intervention, capitalist monopoly. Therefore we say that all the theories advanced by economists about the wage scale, have been invented after the event to justify the existing injustices. We do not need to take them into consideration.

There are those who will tell us that, nevertheless, the collectivist scale of wages would represent an advance: "It will always be better — we shall be told — to have a category of people paid twice or three times as much as the majority of the workers than to have Rothchilds who pocket in a day what the worker does not manage to earn in a year. It would always be a step towards equality."

For us it would be to advance in the wrong direction. In a socialist society to make a distinction between unskilled work and professional work, would mean the revolution agreeing to, and raising to the level of a principle, a brutal fact to which we are at present subjected but which we nevertheless consider to be unjust. It would be doing what those men of August 4th 1789 did, when they proclaimed the abolition of feudal rights in strong, telling, language but who on August 8th were approving those very rights by imposing ground rents on the peasantry, in order to buy them back from the landed gentry. It would be doing like the Russian government, at the time of the emancipation of the serfs, when they proclaimed that the land would henceforth belong to the landed gentry, whereas before it was a breach of trust to dispose of land that belonged to the serfs.

Or again to take a better known example: when the Commune of 1871 decided to pay the members of the Council of the Commune 15 francs a day, whereas the fédérés at the city ramparts only received 30 sous, some welcomed this decision as an act of higher egalitarian democracy. But in reality by this decision, the Commune was agreeing to the former inequality that existed between the bureaucrat and the soldier, the government and the governed. For an opportunist chamber such a decision would have been excellent; but for a commune it was a lie. The commune was lying to its revolutionary principle, and was condemned by that very principle.

One can affirm, grosso modo that the man who throughout his life has deprived himself of leisure for ten hours a day has given to society much more than one who has deprived himself of only five hours, or the one who has not deprived himself of any hours. But one cannot take what he did in two hours and say that the product is worth twice as much as the product of one hour's work by another individual and to remunerate him in proportion. To do so would be to ignore all the complexities of industry and agriculture — the whole existence of society today; it would mean leaving out of account the extent to which all individual work is the result of past and present work of society as a whole. It would be as though one were living in the Stone Age, whereas we are living in the age of steel.

Indeed, take any example — for instance a coal mine — and see if there is the remotest possibility of measuring and evaluating the services rendered by each individual engaged in mining coal.

Take that man, in charge of the huge machine which raises and lowers the cage in a modern mine. He controls a lever which stops and reverses the movement of the machine. He stops the cage and in the twinkling of an eye reverses its course; it hurtles up or down at lightning speed. He observes an indicator on the wall which tells him at every instant at what point the cage is in the pit shaft.

Eyes glued to the indicator, he observes its movement, and once it has reached a certain mark, he suddenly halts the rush of the cage — neither a metre higher nor lower than the agreed level. And no sooner have the coal-wagonnettes been unloaded and the empty ones loaded than he reverses the lever and the cage is once more hurtling downwards. For 8, 10, consecutive hours he performs prodigies of concentration. If he relaxes for a single instant the cage will fly up and shatter the wheels, break the cable, crush the men and bring all work in the mine to a standstill. If he loses three seconds at each movement of the lever then — in the modern pits — output is reduced by anything from 20 to 50 tons a day.

Well, is it he who renders the greatest service in the mine? Or is it perhaps that boy who from below signals to him when it is time to raise the cage to the surface? Is it instead the miner who is risking his life at every moment of the day at the pit face and who will one day be killed by fire-damp explosion? Or again is it the engineer who would miss the coal seam and have the miners dig into stone if he made the smallest error in his calculations?

Or, finally — to quote the economists who also advocate payment according to the "deeds" which they calculate in their own way — is it the mine owner who has sunk all his fortune and who perhaps against all the forecasts has ordered them to "dig here, you will find excellent quality coal."

All the workers engaged in the mine contribute within the limits of their powers, their knowledge, their intelligence and their skill to mine coal. And all we can say is that everybody has the right to *live*, to satisfy their needs, and even their fantasies, once the most pressing needs of all have been satisfied. But how can one estimate their *labours*?

And furthermore, the coal they have extracted is it really *their* labour? Is it not also the labour of those men who built the railways leading to the pithead and the roads that lead in all directions from the stations? Is it not also the work of those who have cultivated and planted the fields, mined the iron ore, felled the timber in the forest, built the machines that will burn the coal and so on?

No distinction can be drawn between the work of any of them. To measure it by the results, leads us into absurdity. To divide them into fractions and measure them by the hours of work, also leads to absurd conclusions. All one can do is not to measure them at all and to recognise the right of all who engage in productive work to enjoy the comforts of life.

But consider a completely different branch of human activity: take the whole of our existence and say who among us can claim a higher reward for his labours? Is it the doctor who has diagnosed the disease or the nurse who has made a recovery possible by her medical care? Is it the inventor of the first steam engine or the boy who, one day, tiring of having to pull the rope which had served to open the valve to admit the steam under the piston, attached the rope to the engine's lever and went off to play with his pals, without realising that he had invented the vital mechanism for all modern engines — the automatic valve? Is it the inventor of the locomotive, or that Newcastle worker who suggested replacing the stones, which had until then been placed under the rails, and which caused the derailment of trains due to a lack of elasticity, by wooden sleepers? Is it the engine driver or the man who with his signals stops the trains or gives them the right of way?

Or again take the transatlantic cable. Who has done most for the benefit of society: the engineer who insisted in maintaining that the cable could transmit telegrams, whereas the academics of the electrical faculty said it was impossible? Or rather Maury, the academic who advised the abandonment of the large cable for one no thicker than a walking stick? Or again, those volunteers who came from no one knows where, who spent night and day on the bridge to examine every inch of cable and remove the nails that the shareholders of the shipping companies had stupidly hired others to drive into the insulating layer of the cable in order to put it out of action?

And in an even wider sphere — the real sphere of human existence with its joys, sorrows and accidents — cannot each one of us name somebody who did one a service so great, so important, that he would be horrified if it was suggested to him to estimate the value of that service in money terms? That service could have been a word, just a word, the right one at the right moment; or it could well have been months and years of devotion. Are you going to evaluate these services, the most important of all in "work tokens?"

"The deeds of each!" — But human societies would not survive two consecutive generations, they would disappear in fifty years if everyone did not give infinitely more than they would receive in money, in "tokens" or in civic awards.

It would be the extinction of the species if a mother did not use her own life to preserve that of her children, if no man gave without charging, if man did not give, above all, when no reward could be expected. And if bourgeois society perishes, if we are today at a dead end from which there is no way out without taking the torch and the axe to the institutions of the past — it is just because one has done too much calculating, which has been just the thing for rogues. It is because we have allowed ourselves to be led to *give* only in order to *receive*, and to have made of society a commercial enterprise based on a *debit* and *credit* accounting.

The collectivists know this anyway. They vaguely understand that a society could not exist if it carried the principle "to each according to his deeds" to its logical conclusions. They realise that the individual's *needs* — we are not talking of luxuries — do not always match up to his deeds.

Thus, De Paepe tells us: "This eminently individualist principle would anyway be tempered by social intervention for the education of children and young people (including maintenance and food) and by social organisations for the care of the sick and infirm, and pensions for elderly workers etc."

They realise that a man of 40, father of three children, has greater needs than a young man of twenty. They realise that the woman who is suckling her baby and spending sleepless nights by its cot cannot perform as many "deeds" as one who has been peacefully sleeping. They seem to understand that the man and woman worn out by perhaps having worked too hard for society in general may find themselves unable to perform as many "deeds" as those who had worked their hours less energetically and pocketed their "tokens" in such privileged situations as State statisticians. And they hasten to *temper* their principle. "But of course" they say, "society will feed and rear its children! But of course it will help the aged and the infirm! But of course the needs and not the *deeds* will be the yardstick of public spending to temper the principle of deeds." Charity — well, well! Charity organised by the State. By improving the foundling hospital, organising insurance schemes against old age and sickness — thus will the principle be tempered!

Thus, then, after having rejected communism, after having sneered at the formula "to each according to his needs" — when it suited them — well I do declare! if they have not also realised that their eminent economists have forgotten something!

Namely the needs of the producers. And so they hasten to recognise them. However it will be the State that will set a value on their services and to decide whether the needs are not disproportionate    to the deeds and to modify them if they are.

It will be left to the State to give alms to whoever is prepared to recognise his inferiority. From that to the poor law and the English workhouse is but a step.

There is but a single step because even this harsh society which disgusts us, has also found itself obliged to temper its principle of individualism. It too has also had to make concessions in a communistic direction and in the same guise of charity.

It too distributes one sou meals to prevent the looting of its shops. It too builds hospitals — often very bad ones though sometimes magnificent ones — to prevent the ravages of contagious dis- eases. It too after having paid no more than the hours of work, takes into care the children of those whom it has reduced to a state of utter destitution. It too takes account of needs — out of charity.

The extreme poverty of the unfortunates — as we have pointed out elsewhere — was the prime cause of riches. It created the first capitalist, for before the "surplus value" which is so much talked about, could be accumulated there had to exist moreover unfortunates who would agree to sell their labour power in order not to die of hunger. It was abject poverty which produced the rich. And if poverty advanced at such a great pace in the course of the Middle Ages, it was above all because of a succession of wars and invasions, the creation of States and the development of their authority; the increase of riches resulting from the exploitation of the Far East, these and many other similar causes, broke the links which formerly united the agrarian and urban communities; and, instead of the solidarity which they once practised, it led them to proclaim the principle of "To hell with needs! And only deeds will be paid for and let everyone solve their problems as best they can!"

And is this the principle that will emerge from the revolution? Is this the principle which they dare to refer to as the social revolution — that term so dear to all the hungry, the sick and the oppressed?

But it will not be so. For when the old institutions crumble beneath the axe of the proletariat, there will be found among them the small groups who will cry out "Bread for all! Lodgings for all! The Right for all to the comforts of life!"

And these voices will be heeded. The people will say to themselves; "Let us begin by satisfying our needs of life, joy and freedom. And once all will have experienced this well-being we will set to work to demolish the last vestiges of the bourgeois regime, its morality, derived from the account book, its philosophy of "debit" and "credit," its institutions of mine and thine. And in demolishing we shall build as Proudhon used to say. But we shall build on new foundations — of communism and anarchy and not of individualism and authority.

# 'WHO WILL DO THE DIRTY WORK?'

*Tony Gibson*

*Tony Gibson (1914-2001), famed as the face of Brylcreem and jailed as a conscientious objector in the 1940s, later became a psychologist. He was a frequent contributor to* Freedom *newspaper until shortly before his death and an exponent of the philosophy of Max Stirner. This essay was first published as an eight-page pamphlet by Freedom Press in 1952.*

Everyone who speaks on the subject of anarchism meets the ever-recurring question. "But in a social condition of anarchy, who will clean out the sewers?" There are variants of the question; sometimes the enquiry concerns those who will do the hardest work or the dirtiest work, but generally the sewers are mentioned specifically. It would seem that everyone wants to be sure that he will not have to work in the sewers in a free society. Perhaps the capitalist and authoritarian status quo derives the apathetic support it does conditional on the fact that only a tiny fraction of the working-class are economically forced to work in the sewers. I have had no contact with sewer-workers myself; perhaps, not having had the usual bogey before them, they are unafraid of the coming social revolution, for, after all, they work in the sewers, anyway.

I have for many years evaded this haunting question when speaking to public audiences, for I am convinced that the real motive that prompts it must be left to the psychoanalysts, who could tell us quite a lot about the basis of this sewer-dread in the unconscious mind. I feel that sense of embarrassment that we all feel when we are in danger of unearthing someone else's pet neurosis. However, I am now prepared to treat the question, in print, as though it were a rational one.

Before considering who, in fact, will clean out the sewers and do other work that is generally considered "dirty," in a free society, let us first consider who does it now. Let us also enquire into the nature of "dirty work." The people who are now concerned with "dirty work" are sewer-cleaners, dustmen, surgeons, housewives, slaughter-house men, hospital nurses, lawyers, soldiers, farmers, politicians, tannery workers, gutter-journalists, etc, etc. The first main distinction we may make is between those who can wash off the dirt of their trade at the end of the day's work, and those who cannot. Dirty work is not to everyone's taste. The smells of the sewer or tannery would revolt some people; others would be revolted by the things a surgeon, nurse or slaughter-house man does; others would prefer to do either of these things than touch the filth that lies in the province of the lawyer, politician and gutter-journalist. Our tastes vary.

What is notable about these different occupations is that some are highly paid and some poorly paid.

This makes a great difference in our money-conscious society, but perhaps the social prestige attached to the job carries even more weight with many people. A great number of men would rather slave away at an underpaid clerking job with no hope of advancement than undertake the healthier and better paid work of dock-worker. Many girls will work ten hours a day toting bed-pans and dressing wounds rather than take work as a bar-maid. The question of pay and of the "dirtiness" of work does not always override considerations of social esteem (often called snobbery).

For a short while I happened to be cleaning the streets of Cardiff for my living; while attending an intellectual gathering a lady asked me what my work was. I told her. Perhaps she was right in thinking that I wished to be rude to her by telling her the truth. Had I wished to play up to the occasion and avoid paining her, I would have vaguely replied that I worked in an important occupation for the benefit of the municipality.

I have read with interest of the shift of social prestige connected with work in the newly organised state of Israel. There, owing to the peculiar nature of the immigrants, there is a huge surplus of professional men. Lawyers, doctors, professors, architects, etc, are far too numerous and there is no living to be made by the majority of them, but bricklayers, navvies, agricultural workers, etc, are in huge demand.

Manual work therefore commands a high wage, and the professional men are taking to it, but the important shift of emphasis is that now jobs that make your hands dirty are socially approved in Israel, in contrast to the social contempt in which such work is held in other capitalist countries.

No doubt if capitalism persists in Israel the situation will deteriorate to match other countries, but while it lasts it is an interesting exposition of how a social attitude can quickly change towards "dirty work."

## Coercion as the Root of Evils

It has been pointed out time and again that in a sanely organised society there would be no problem of work which is intrinsically dirty, revolting and degrading. Such things as garbage collection, sewage disposal, rag picking, furnace stoking, etc, are unpleasant operations in contemporary society only because those employed in them have not the power to alter their conditions of work.

If there were not powerless and exploited beings who must accept filthy and unpleasant conditions of work, as there are today, these operations would have priority for the best scientific research and technical skill to be applied to them to make them not merely acceptable as occupations, but congenial. For the key to social harmony lies in the relation of human beings to their work. I would define a free society (that is a health society) as one in which there is no social coercion compelling the individual to work.

This definition of anarchy may call forth considerable protest from some anarchists, but I mean it in its most literal sense.

Superficially, such an idea seems completely unrealistic, and to be dismissed out of hand as foolish idealism by those who have some experience of life. Let me disassociate myself from all idealism.

I have had practical experience of idealists who had such faith in and love of "Man" that they would let themselves by exploited by work-shy layabouts rather than face the fact that they were supporting parasites to no good purpose.

But I also want to make it clear that there is no freedom, nor stability, nor health in any community of people, large or small, where the socially necessary work is carried out merely from a sense of social duty which is imposed upon the individual. The only justification for work is the fact that we enjoy it. Any society which relies upon political, economic or moral coercion as the mainspring of its productive process is doomed to unhealth and some form of servitude.

Work may be defined as the expenditure of energy in a productive process, as distinct from play which is the expenditure of energy without productive result. Work is characteristic of the healthy adult being, play of the healthy child whose energies are occupied in developing his own capacities.

Significantly enough, the play of the children of humans, and of other mammals, is generally a rehearsal of adult work-activities.

It is generally realised that work is a necessity for every adult. Those people who have no economic need to work, by reason of their wealth, have to seek work-substitutes to preserve their mental and physical health. They remain, as it were, permanent children, playing at fishing, hunting, sailing boats, gardening and farming, and often find satisfaction in quite strenuous work-play.

The lower mammals are no different from humans; they need to work when they are adult. Being less troubled by intellectual doubt, they pursue their occupations with wholehearted satisfaction.

In studying creatures simpler than ourselves there can be no doubt as to what gives them pleasure: the otter likes to fish, the beaver to build dams, the squirrel to collect nuts, the rabbit to burrow.

Some people may point to their domestic Pussy, "corrupted by a thousand years of unnatural living," who prefers to lap milk by the fireside than to hunt mice in the cellar, and draw the analogy that modern man is an unnatural animal and needs to be kicked before he will work.

In this common analogy there is a biological fallacy. Neither Pussy, nor you, nor I, is 1,000 years old: we are not instinctually conditioned by the experiences of our ancestors. We have a certain instinctual endowment which is pretty much the same as when our species first originated, and our behaviour is conditioned by the environment we encounter in our own life span.

Turn pampered Pussy loose in the woods and she will revert to a natural feline way of life; remove the pressure of neurotic twentieth-century civilisation from you and I and we will have the chance of reverting to a natural human way of life which, I contend, includes as spontaneous a wish for and enjoyment of work as the way of life of any other animal species.

At present, many of the civilised varieties of our species appear to be unique in the animal kingdom in that their productive process expresses no joy of life. The position is even worse than this: we take it for granted that all animals enjoy the procreative process, but among many of our species even this function has lost its pleasure.

Do we have to look further for the roots of all the social disharmony and individual misery of our time? With us, work is generally regarded as a regrettable necessity, an activity to be endured only for the sake of the material goods produced, or rather for the wage packet which bears no obvious relationship to the work done. The best that the reformers, social planners and even social revolutionaries can suggest is that we may make the working day shorter, so that there will be less pain (work) and more pleasure (idleness) in our lives. I have even heard an anarchist meeting discussing whether in the great and glorious by-and-by we should have to do three hours work a day or three hours work a week.

This is strictly comparable to the following extract from an American sex-instruction manual: "Question. How long does the penis have to stay in the vagina? "Answer. Only a few minutes." Another regrettable necessity!

I do not care if in a social state of anarchy we work a great deal longer than we do today under capitalism. What I am concerned about is that the work itself shall be intrinsically satisfying. I see no other way of ensuring this than the abandonment of coercion as the mainspring of production.

It is obvious that if the wages-system, which is the chief coercive force compelling men to work at their present jobs today, were to break down, the following situation would arise. A large number of people would be liberated but disorientated, and they would immediately take the attitude of, "From now on it's spiv and live for me — only mugs work!" This is to be expected. Domesticated Pussy when first turned loose in the woods looks around for another house to sponge off; she does not immediately take on a natural feline way of life.

It is this situation that most social revolutionaries are afraid of, and they seek to set up authoritarian machinery to substitute political coercion for the economic coercion of capitalism. It is true that political coercion is not always easy to apply to the productive processes; under Lenin's dictatorship it was largely abandoned for the economic coercion of the New Economic Policy.

However, if coercion is still resorted to after the breakdown of capitalism in order that men will still work, the "spiv and live" attitude will be preserved as a permanent social attitude.

The problem is not one of "faith" in human nature, it is one of understanding. Either one realises that human beings are social animals with basically sound animal instincts for self-preservation, or one does not. Those who do not realise the potential animal idealised concept of man, and take it for granted that Tom, Dick and Harry must be bludgeoned into working, eating, sleeping, bedding with their wives, and cleaning their teeth in the approved manner or they will die from lack of knowing what Man should be.

Tom, Dick and Harry are not always pretty creatures, but they are generally better social specimens than the do-gooders, the dangerous fools who would accept the responsibility for organising their lives for them.

It is my purpose to draw particular attention to the anti-social nature of conscientious administrators. We all know about the harmful nature of conscious exploiters and racketeers under so-called laissez-faire capitalism, but it is the prophets of planned economy and super-government who are the harbingers of famine, war and desolation for the future.

## Breaking with Custom

If through a revolutionary breakdown of capitalist society, the compulsion to go to the accustomed place of wage-slavery is no longer operative, then the disorientated people will have the chance to turn to production for use to satisfy their own needs for work. It is usually assumed that the great problem is what ulterior incentives or compulsions to work must be instituted to satisfy the demands of the consumers.

We tend to forget that it is as natural for men to produce as to consume. In any society where the producers of wealth are not subject to coercion, the demands of the consumers must follow what it is the nature of that society to produce, every adult being both producer and consumer.

That this is hard for many people to realise, I know, for we are accustomed to think of there being a class of "workers" in society, whose function it is to do as they are told. If the "consumers" demand televisions, battleships, Coca Cola and coal, then the "workers" have no say in the matter — they must produce them. It is time we tried to conceive a society without the coercion of worker by consumer, for as long as we have this picture engraved on our minds it is impossible to think in terms of practical anarchy.

Anarchist writers have dealt at length with the fact that only a very small percentage of the people in this country are really producing anything useful or performing any socially useful function whatever, in spite of the vast degree of unpleasant activity around us. A gross dislocation of our industry would not therefore be a calamity at all.

We need a breakdown of the present industrial system; we need revolution and real anarchy in which to reorganise our productive processes with workers in control of their work and motivated by their own need to work, instead of their need of a pay-packet.

The worst calamity that can take place after the breakdown of capitalism is the replacement of economic coercion by political coercion. We are already experiencing the thin edge of the wedge.

Those workers who are no longer on the economic border of destitution sometimes choose to stay away from work. As the economic bludgeon fails to intimidate them, the State has recourse to the political bludgeon, and criminal proceedings are taken. How else would you coerce men to work?

Either, the individual must be free to go to work or stay away, and society can lump it, or society must preserve its coercive machinery, the State. Anarchism is based on the recognition of the fact that, in freedom, men will choose to work.

"But surely some workers, the workers concerned with essential services — cleaning the sewers for instance — must be made to carry out their work, even under anarchy!"

Will you go down and clean out those sewers for the sake of society, madam? No? Then, madam, you may have to use the yard. Or perhaps you will find that many people are less squeamish than you, and will take more interest in disposing of your sewage efficiently, hygienically and usefully than you do yourself. They may even send it back to you in the form of properly grown vegetables.

# THE DOMINANT IDEA

*Voltairine De Cleyre*

*De Cleyre (1866-1912) became one of the most prolific and prominent anarchist agitators in US anarchism after being converted to the ideology in the wake of the Haymarket Affair in 1887, in which eight anarchists were infamously fitted up for conspiring to bomb a Chicago rally. She wrote extensively, being described by historian Paul Avrich as "a greater literary talent than any other American anarchist." De Cleyre originally contributed this piece to Emma Goldman's publication Mother Earth, which published it in 1910.*

I think there is no one in the world who can look upon the steadfast, far-staring face of an Egyptian carving, or read a description of Egypt's monuments, or gaze upon the mummied clay of its old dead men, without feeling that the dominant idea of that people in that age was to be enduring and to work enduring things, with the immobility of their great still sky upon them and the stare of the desert in them.

One must feel that whatever other ideas animated them, and expressed themselves in their lives, this was the dominant idea. That which was must remain, no matter at what cost, even if it were to break the ever-lasting hills: an idea which made the live humanity beneath it, born and nurtured in the corns of caste, groan and writhe and gnaw its bandages, till in the fullness of time it passed away: and still the granite mould of it stares with empty eyes out across the world, the stern old memory of the *Thing-that-was*.

I think no one can look upon the marbles wherein Greek genius wrought the figuring of its soul without feeling an apprehension that the things are going to leap and fly; that in a moment one is like to be set upon by heroes with spears in their hands, by serpents that will coil around him; to be trodden by horses that may trample and flee; to be smitten by these gods that have as little of the idea of stone in them as a dragon-fly, one instant poised upon a wind-swayed petal edge.

I think no one can look upon them without realising at once that those figures came out of the boil of life; they seem like rising bubbles about to float into the air, but beneath them other bubbles rising, and others, and others — there will be no end of it. When one's eyes are upon one group, one feels that behind one, perhaps, a figure is tiptoeing to seize the darts of the air and hurl them on one's head; one must keep whirling to face the miracle that appears about to be wrought — stone leaping! And this though nearly every one is minus some of the glory the old Greek wrought into it so long ago; even the broken stumps of arms and legs live.

And the dominant idea is activity, and the beauty and strength of it. Change, swift, ever-circling change! The making of things and the casting of them away, as children cast away their toys, not interested that these shall endure, so that they themselves realise incessant activity.

Full of creative power what matter if the creature perished. So there was an endless procession of changing shapes in their schools, their philosophies their dramas, their poems, till at last it wore itself to death. And the marvel passed away from the world. But still their marbles live to show what manner of thoughts dominated them.

And if we wish to know what master-thought ruled the lives of men when the medieval period had had time to ripen it, one has only at this day to stray into some quaint, out-of-the-way English village, where a strong old towered church yet stands in the midst of little straw-thatched cottages, like a brooding mother-hen surrounded by her chickens. Everywhere the greatening of God and the lessening of man: the church so looming, the home so little. The search for the spirit, for the *enduring* thing (not the poor endurance of granite which in the ages crumbles, but the eternal), the eternal, — and contempt for the body which perishes, manifest in studied uncleanliness, in mortifications of the flesh, as if the spirit should have spat its scorn upon it.

Such was the dominant idea of that Middle Age which has been too much cursed by modernists. For the men who built the castles and the cathedrals, were men of mighty works, though they made no books, and though their souls spread crippled wings, because of their very endeavors to soar too high. The spirit of voluntary subordination for the accomplishment of a great work, which proclaimed the aspiration of the common soul, — that was the spirit wrought into the cathedral stones; and it is not wholly to be condemned.

In waking dream, when the shadow-shapes of world-ideas swim before the vision, one sees the Middle Age soul, an ill-contorted, half-formless thing, with dragon wings and a great, dark, tense face, strained sunward with blind eyes.

If now we look around us to see what idea dominates our own civilisation, I do not know that it is even as attractive as this piteous monster of the old darkness. The relativity of things has altered: man has risen and God has descended. The modern village has better homes and less pretentious churches. Also, the conception of dirt and disease as much-sought afflictions, the patient suffering of which is a meet offering to win God's pardon, has given place to the emphatic promulgation of cleanliness.

We have public school nurses notifying parents that "pediculosis capitis" is a very contagious and unpleasant disease; we have cancer associations gathering up such cancers as have attached themselves to impecunious persons, and carefully experimenting with a view to cleaning them out of the human race; we have tuberculosis societies attempting the Herculean labour of clearing the Aegean stables of our modern factories of the deadly bacillus, and they have got as far as spittoons with water in them in some factories; and others, and others, and others, which while not yet overwhelmingly successful in their avowed purposes are evidence sufficient that humanity no longer seeks dirt as a means of grace.

We laugh at those old superstitions and talk much about exact experimental knowledge. We endeavor to galvanise the Greek corpse, and pretend that we enjoy physical culture.

We dabble in many things; but the one great real idea of our age, not copied from any other, not pretended, not raised to life by any conjuration, is the Much Making of Things, — not the making of beautiful things, not the joy of spending living energy in creative work; rather the shameless, merciless driving and over-driving, wasting and draining of the last lit of energy, only to produce heaps and heaps of things — things ugly, things harmful, things useless, and at the best largely unnecessary.

To what end are they produced? Mostly the producer does not know; still less does he care. But he is possessed with the idea that he must do it, every one is doing it, and every year the making of things goes on more and faster; there are mountain ranges of things made and making, and still men go about desperately seeking to increase the list of created things, to start fresh heaps and to add to the existing heaps.

And with what agony of body, under what stress and strain of danger and fear of danger, with what mutilations and maimings and lamings they struggle on, dashing themselves out against these rocks of wealth! Verily, if the vision of the medieval soul is painful in its blind staring and pathetic striving, grotesque in its senseless tortures, the soul of the modern is most amazing with its restless, nervous eyes, ever searching the corners of the universe, its restless, nervous hands ever reaching and grasping for some useless toil.

# ALTERNATIVES AND FUTURES

## REFLECTIONS ON UTOPIA

*SP*

*The writer of the article lived for 18 months in a kibbutz (1948-50) and revisited it in 1962, the same year in which this essay was written. Invited to write a postscript in 1983, his reaction was that it did not need one because "nothing has changed radically" apart from the fact that most have become "richer" but "the money goes into higher living standards or the creation of new industries etc. He concludes that the kibbutz, some of which are now "more than 70 years old with a third generation of children" are "still valid as a microcosm of what larger units like villages or small towns could be in a sensible world."*

Of all the experiments conducted in the last 100 years the kibbutz or collective in Israel occupies a unique position. If only by virtue of its longevity it tends to suggest that people are in fact capable of living a new way of life, differing radically from life in the outside world. It poses many problems while attempting to answer many more that plague the man outside. It is one of the best examples of democracy and certainly the nearest thing to practising anarchism that exists. Every pet theory of anarchism, like decentralisation, minority opinion, "law" without government, freedom and not licence, delegation of representation are all part of the daily pattern of existence.

Here in microcosm may be seen the beginnings of what might happen in a genuinely free society. It would be ludicrous to suggest that it is internally a problemless life, or that perfection is round the corner. But what it does suggest is that people are capable sometimes, in spite of themselves, of being responsible and rational in the conduct of their lives.

Though these collectives have grown out of very specific conditions they are not exclusive in the sense that no Englishman or Frenchman would be incapable of living in such a manner. The ideas that motivated their origins were socialist in content and, although adverse environmental factors and geographical difficulties might at that time have forced an intenser communal spirit, when these conditions got better in later years the collectivist spirit has remained as strong as ever.

Basically the whole structure works very simply. Each department works independently through part of an overall plan approved each year by the community as a whole, usually through a general meeting. Each department has a head, usually elected by the department itself. These are not permanent positions, re-election takes place each year, and each head works on the job as do all the others, but he may make decisions based upon experience. Decisions made by heads or any plan for development must be submitted for general approval, while any elected member may find himself removed from office should there be any evidence of malpractice or incompetence.

No decision is ever carried if there remains a substantial minority of opinion in opposition. The issue is left in abeyance till more discussion can take place and unanimity can be reached.

There is no money in the internal life of the community. All food, clothing, houses, health and social security are dealt with by the various committees concerned with these problems. The approach is personal. One is not talking to an official, but to a friend of yours, probably living next door.

There is no governing body, and no written laws, though a hazy identification with socialist principles seems to be commonly held. Equality has a meaning in everyday life, and this often produces one of the problems of the new society.

Social pressure is the only effective deterrent to anti-social behaviour, and the only one in use. It works subtly, and no-one is ever brought to account, but the knowledge that such a force exists seems to be sufficient.

There is no crime in these communities, and therefore no police, law courts and prisons. There is no private property and no inheritance, and possessiveness takes on a different form from that which we know. This cultivated "instinct" to possess often finds expression in a kind of pride in the community's possessions; such impersonal things as a modern milking parlour or an all-automatic washing-up machine. There is also some justifiable pride in achievement like "making the desert bloom," etc.

All basic things are owned communally, though people do live in their own houses for as long as they remain members. Clothes and personal articles are the only private property allowed in the sense that we know it.

Children live in their own separate age communities, within the community. Each age group numbers approximately 18, with not less than three teachers to a group.

The children live, etc., play and are educated in their own community, and visit their parents after work. Even the babies live apart from the parents after breast feeding is over. Children refer to their teachers by their first names, and punishment of any kind is unknown.

Talent is always encouraged, and communities will send any child for further education in their specific inclinations to courses in town, or even overseas. All monetary transactions with the outside world are done by the community treasurer. Though when any member has his annual leave, and goes into town, he gets a lump sum for his two weeks expenses.

Work is allocated to each member by a committee, who are determined by the specific need of the community or by the special project on hand. Individual consideration will play a part in the final allocation of jobs. One can object, and, if one has a good case to present, one can have one's job changed.

At first sight it seems an ideal democracy. Authority is so spread out, and each individual member so intimately involved in all that goes on, that one can think of no better way of conducting economic life. These kibbutzim may vary in numbers from 200 to 2,000, and a great deal of organisation is involved in housing and feeding such numbers.

As suggested earlier in this article it is as yet not the ideal society. Though few could quarrel with the ideological basis of such communities, there are many problems that need to be tackled. All this would be of interest to those who tend to create "free societies" in their more contemplative moments, or at public meetings.

The greatest problem is perhaps the necessary re-education that members have to undergo to accept the abolition of personal possessions. This is contrary to all our upbringing in an acquisitive society such as ours. To many in our society possession equals security. The change is often hard. Also, living close to people often involves one in their problems, sometimes inescapably so. Whereas in London one often hears of people lying dead in their rooms for six weeks before their neighbours find them, such non-interest in one's fellows cannot exist in a kibbutz.

The children appear to be self-confident and independent, with little evidence of that sticky child-parent relationship so obvious elsewhere. This relationship is often a bone of contention with educationalists and self-regulators and other theoreticians of child upbringing, who sometimes tend to over-protect their children, or attempt to live their lives through their offspring. Perhaps the first test of the community will come when this new generation grows up. Will it reproduce this new way of life, or will it return to that which their parents had rejected? The bright lights and the apparent freedom of the city still exert some allure to both young and old, and, though many have solved this problem, the new generation must still handle it.

This writer found that political indoctrination, or bias perhaps might be a better term for it, to be one of the negative aspects of these communities. Their defence is that a community cannot just be an "ivory tower," but must make itself felt in the world around it. No attempt has been made here to discuss the political affiliations of the communities, or their relationship to the state, or to the heavy financial debt that most of the communities are in. There is much that one can say about the influence of the outside world. The kibbutz does not live in isolation, yet within its walls it retains a unique system of social relationships, an environment where new ideas and individual talent will be encouraged. Here, as long as one chooses to remain a member, one can have a real sense of belonging, with a system of social security unequalled anywhere else in the world, and to some degree a feeling of personal usefulness and status. Within its confines no man can be exploited by another, and no man is occupied in unnecessary and unproductive labour. The work each man does has dignity and is recognised.

Yet it cannot be a life for all. It conflicts strongly with authoritarian upbringing. Fierce individualism would find its confines too narrow, its politics no better than elsewhere in the world. Yet it reflects both the limitation and the aspirations of a better way of life.

# COLLECTIVES IN THE SPANISH REVOLUTION

Gaston Leval

*Some of the "Final Reflections" in Leval's monumental study of* Collectives in the Spanish Revolution. *An English translation was published by Freedom Press in 1975.*

One of the dominant characteristics which impresses whoever studies the Spanish Revolution is its many-sidedness. This revolution was guided by certain very clear and very definite principles, which involved the general expropriation of the holders of social wealth, the seizure by the workers of the organisational structures of production and distribution, the direct administration of public services, the establishment of the libertarian communist principle. But the uniformity of these principles did not prevent a diversity in the methods for their application, so much so that one can talk of "diversity within unity" and of a surprisingly diversified federalism.

In a very short time, in the agrarian regions and especially in Aragon, a new organism appeared: the collective. Nobody had spoken about it before. The three instruments of social reconstruction foreseen among those libertarians who had expressed themselves on a possible future were firstly the syndicate, then the cooperative, which did not win many supporters, and finally, on a rather large scale, the commune, or communal organisation. Some foreshadowed — and this writer was among them — that a new and complementary organism could and should appear, especially in the countryside, seeing that the syndicate had not assumed the importance it had in the towns, and the kind of life, of work and production, did not fit into an organic monolithic structure which was contrary to the multiformity of daily life.

We have seen how that collective was born with characteristics of its own. It is not the syndicate, for it encompasses all those who wish to join it whether they are producers in the classic economic sense or not. Then it brings them together at the complete human individual level and not just at a craft level. Within it, from the first moment, the rights and duties are the same for everybody; there are no longer professional categories in mutual opposition making the producers into privileged consumers compared with those, such as housewives, who are not producers in the classical definition of the word.

Neither is the collective the municipal council or what is called the commune, the municipality. For it parts company with the political party traditions on which the commune is normally based. It encompasses at the same time the syndicate and municipal functions. It is all-embracing. Each of its activities is organised within its organism, and the whole population takes part in its management, whether it is a question of a policy for agriculture, for the creation of new industries, for social solidarity, medical service or public education.

In this general activity the collective brings each and everybody to an awareness of life in the round, and everyone to the practical necessity of mutual understanding.

Compared with the collective the syndicate has simply a secondary or subordinate role. It is striking to observe how in the agricultural districts, it was more often than not spontaneously relegated, almost forgotten, in spite of the efforts that the libertarian-syndicalists and the anarcho-syndicalists had previously made. The collective replaced them. The word itself was born spontaneously and spread into all the regions of Spain where the agrarian revolution had been brought about. And the word "collectivist" was adopted just as quickly and spread with the same spontaneity.

One could advance the hypothesis that these two words — collective and collectivism — better expressed the people's moral, human, fraternal feelings than did the terms syndicates and syndicalism. A question of euphony perhaps, and of a breadth of views, of humanism: man as something more than the producer. The need for syndicates no longer exists when there are no more employers.

If we pass from Aragon to the Levante we see collectives emerging there too but not as such a spontaneous, one might almost say instant, creation. It was the agricultural and sometimes the non-agricultural, syndicates which were there at the beginning, not to found other syndicates, and this is most significant, but *to found collectives*. And those who joined these collectives, often without belonging to the syndicates, were also collectivists and acted and behaved as well as anybody else. Let us hasten to add that the groups of organisers often consisted of men who had until then been active in the syndicates or even in libertarian groups.

But there were some cases where the commune fulfilled the role of the collective. Among the examples we have given, one especially recalls Granollers, Hospitalet, Fraga, Binefar, and many places in Castile. We also find municipalities which had been reconstructed to conform with governmental decisions (January 1937) and had, as a result, played a more or less important, more or less subordinate, role; and in the Levante the syndicate and the collective in the end linked their activities. But in that region the role of the syndicate was often to become more important, both through direct participation and as inspirer and guide, which it was not in Aragon.

Finally we see in Castile, the collectives being started in large numbers under the impulse of militant workers and even intellectuals who left Madrid and spread out into the countryside.

This plasticity, this variety of ways of acting allowed for the creation of true socialism, in each place according to the situation, circumstances of time and place, and for the resolution of a great number of problems which an authoritarian concept, too rigid, too bureaucratic would have only made more complicated with, in the end, a dictatorship reducing everything to a uniform pattern. The variety of methods used reflected the variety of the facets of life.

Often in the same region, villages with similar forms of production, with a somewhat similar social history, would start by socialising the local industries and end with agriculture, while others would start with the socialisation of agriculture and end with that of local industries. In some cases, in the Levante for instance, we have seen it start with distribution then proceed towards socialisation of production, which was the opposite procedure to most other places.

But it is remarkable that this diversity of organisational structures did not prevent membership of the same regional federations nor, through them, national coordination, practical solidarity, whether it concerned our collectives, mixed syndical collectives or communities at different stages of municipalisation.

The general law was universal solidarity. We have underlined, in passing that the charters or statutes in which the principles were defined and from which stemmed the practical attitude of each and all, made no mention of the rights and liberty of the individual. Not that the collectives had ignored these rights, but simply because the respect of these rights went without saying, and that they were already recognised by the standard of life guaranteed to everybody, in their access to consumer goods, to well-being and culture, to the attention, consideration and *human responsibilities* of which each one, as a member of the collective, was assured. It was known, so why mention it? In return, for this to be possible, everyone had to carry out his duty, do his work like the other comrades, show solidarity according to the ethic of a universal mutual aid.

One was the guarantee of the other. It is for this reason we so often read that same sentence in the charters though there had been no previous discussion between collectives hundreds of kilometres apart: "Anyone not having any work in his trade will help comrades in other activities who might need his help." This was supra-professional solidarity in practice.

Going deeply into these matters it could perhaps be said that they were developing a new concept of liberty. In the village collectives in their natural state, and in the small towns where everybody knew one another and were interdependent, liberty did not consist in being a parasite, and not interesting oneself in anything. Liberty only existed as a function of practical activity. To be is to do, Bakunin wrote. To be is to *realise*, voluntarily. Liberty is secured not only when one demands the rights of the "self" against others, but when it is a natural consequence of solidarity. Men who are interdependent feel free among themselves and naturally respect each other's liberty. Furthermore, so far as collective life is concerned, the freedom of each is the right to participate spontaneously with one's thought, one's heart, one's will, one's initiative to the full extent of one's capacities. A negative liberty is not liberty: it is nothingness.

This concept of liberty gave rise to a new morality — unless it was this new ethic that gave rise to another concept of liberty. It explains why when the author sought information about changes, and improvements introduced in the lives of everyone, they did not speak of "liberty" though they were libertarians, but, and they did so with deep joy, of the results of their work, experiments, and research on which they were engaged;

on the increase in production. No, they were no longer thinking of liberty in the way workers in capitalist factories or day workers of the land of the owner-employer think.

On this subject we would like to make an observation to which we attach great philosophical and practical importance. The theoreticians and partisans of the liberal economy affirm that competition stimulates initiative and, consequently, the creative spirit and invention without which it remains dormant. Numerous observations made by the writer in the collectives, factories and socialised workshops permit him to take quite the opposite view. For in a collective, in a grouping where each individual is stimulated by the wish to be of service to his fellow beings, research, the desire for technical perfection and so on are also stimulated. But they also have as a consequence that other individuals join those who were the first to get together. Furthermore when, in present society, an individualist inventor discovers something, it is used only by the capitalist or the individual employing him, whereas in the case of an inventor living in a community not only is his discovery taken up and developed by others, but is immediately applied for the common good. I am convinced that this superiority would very soon manifest itself in a socialised society.

# SIGNIFICANCE OF THE "SELF-BUILD" MOVEMENT

*First published in* Freedom *May 17 1952. Author unknown.*

We have discussed several times in Freedom the growing movement for "self-building" houses. In a broadcast talk on *Building One's Own House* last month, Mr Fello Atkinson, the architect, said:

> It is a sign of the fearful complication of our times that building one's own house should seem a new idea. What else did our remote ancestors do? And, of course, all primitive and pioneer communities build this way. Grandma Moses, that astonishing ninety-four-year-old American lady who has achieved such fame as a folk painter in the last few years, records in her memoirs how, in her young days, the men of New England wanting to set up home were given land and an axe and set about making their own log cabins. I am certain there are many places where the same thing still happens. The idea is certainly not new but only unusual in modern, highly industrialised communities where each of us, except possibly farmers and sailors, tends to specialise in ever-narrowing fields to the exclusion and even ignorance of all others. The responsibility for housing has now largely passed to government, and there exists a complicated and rigid pattern of planning and building permits, regulations and standards, financing and subsidies.
>
> But, in spite of this, groups of men are building their own houses in this country today; they have been doing so for some time, and they are building them successfully within this complex mechanism. And these 'self-build groups', as they are called, are growing in number.

He went on to describe the activities of groups affiliated to the National Federation of Housing Societies.

This called forth (and it is an indication of the spread of "self-building"), a letter in the *Listener* from the secretary of a group, who wanted to draw attention to the 194 "self-build" groups affiliated to the London and National Self-Build Housing Association, Birmingham, and to "the difficulties and heartbreak of other groups, already fully trained, with considerable financial resources, who have been ready to build for eighteen months, and who lack one thing only — the cooperation of their local authorities to grant the necessary permission for them to go ahead and build."

The writer has also paid tribute to the founders of the associations, who "without any prompting, and for no personal gain, have come forward and shown us, for the first time in our lives, how to help ourselves." For the first time in our lives, how to help ourselves. This is why we believe the "self-building" movement to be so valuable and important.

# LEISURE IN AMERICA

August Heckscher II

*This is an abridged version of a paper delivered in 1961. Heckscher (1913-1997), a former editorial writer for the* New York Herald Tribune, *was at the time Director of the Twentieth Century Fund and became the first White House cultural advisor under Kennedy in 1962-3.*

It is curious, that in the modern history of freedom, leisure has rarely figured as one of its elements. The philosophers have almost invariably been concerned with political freedom; even so, one would have thought that the time in which a citizen could theoretically do as he pleased, without constraint, would count as a determining factor. It has been argued that the citizen was free when he was pursuing his own interests — those interests usually being economic in nature. But the thought that to be free was to be at leisure — to be able, in Emerson's phrase, "to saunter and sit and be inferior and silly" — was really not entertained. For the freedom that springs from leisure one must go back to the Greeks; and they, characteristically, spoke not so much either of freedom or leisure, but of virtue and the good life.

In the end we shall all perhaps have to make ourselves students of the Greeks in these matters. With a more modest aim in view, it is enough for the moment to inquire into the degree to which free time is free in itself — open to the various choices of the mind and heart. Time away from the job is obviously pre-empted in part by many factors. The need to eat and sleep cuts into free time. The chores of home are inevitable and can be time-consuming. There are other factors which are not written into man's lot, but seem to be part of the way our society is organised. The time expended in getting to and from work has tended to increase greatly, and except in the rarest cases these hours can hardly be considered "free." For some the chance to play cards with a regular group of friends riding homeward on the 5.32, or to read or doze, may be one of the pleasantest periods of the day. For most, the journey to and from work is a frustrating experience which they vow they will one day find the means to avoid.

The impression seems inescapable that people alternate between periods of rather complete emptiness and passivity on the one hand, and periods when they are acting under various forms of necessity or compulsion. From watching television aimlessly or enduring grudgingly the disarray and noisiness of family life, the individual flees to various forms of semi-obligatory tasks. Sometimes he finds escape in a formal second job; sometimes in so-called voluntary activities, which actually impose their demands as insistently as any for which pay is being received. A middle area, where men and women find themselves agreeably engaged amid manageable things — neither under compulsion nor pressure, not confused or hurried — is what seems missing in free time today.

Subtracting from hours off the job those that are obviously not free, we may ask ourselves what are the characteristics of free time at its best. It cannot mean time at which our momentary whim is completely in control of our activities. It cannot mean wholly unstructured time, when we wander without any bounds or limits. In every lifetime, and particularly in youth and old age, there is need for such idleness or contemplation; but the times that in the main are most free are those in which we find ourselves engaged in what we have chosen, with some attainable objective in view and some rough pattern to govern our endings and beginnings.

Hobbies can fulfil this function; so can do-it-yourself activities, participation in civic activities, sports, travel, even shopping and cooking. I can say they can fulfil the function of freedom. Too often they do not; for they are undertaken with a sense of compulsiveness and without any clear conviction that what we are doing at one moment is any more profitable or enjoyable than what we are doing at another.

The quality of free time — the degree of freedom that it contains — depends upon characteristics both of the individual citizen and of society at large. The conformist is never free — not because he happens to be doing the same thing as others, but because he is doing it for reasons which have no relation to his inner being. There is a widespread feeling that leisure creates the very conformity which it should have the effect of abolishing. How can this be? If leisure is freedom, and freedom is to follow an inner bent, how does it result in people copying one another and trying to be as similar as possible?

Worry about conformity is not new. When Americans were a people still wholly devoted to the gospel of work, it was regularly complained that we tended to wear the same clothes, hold similar opinions and pursue convergent goals. Now that the gospel of work is largely replaced by the newer gospel of leisure, the complaint continues to be heard.

There may well be in the American a strain of conformism; and this may find expression in one period as readily as the next. Leisure to a large extent is merely a way of expressing ourselves. The soul, to quote Emerson once more, is the colour of its leisure thoughts. But the coming of leisure to a society does nevertheless in some measure change it; and it is worth inquiring with some precision as to whether in our society leisure has accentuated new traits in the citizenry.

If we grow more conformist under leisure, if your free time becomes steadily less free, it may be because the range of choice opened to us is so wide as to be dazzling and to drive us back toward reliance upon external standards. In a society of work the citizens all knew what their roles were supposed to be. They had a certain status and were expected to behave in certain ways, to live in certain types of houses and follow certain pleasures. Work kept people from coalescing, imposing its own discipline upon their lives, creating a variety of skills and routines. But with the relaxation of work standards, people found themselves at sea. They were supposed to know what they wanted to do. But not being very sure they knew, they found it safest to follow the course others had set.

The difficulties of adjusting to a society of abundant free time cannot be over estimated. To grow up in it is to have no convincing image of what life is to be. While the emphasis on success still exerts a powerful influence, the ways in which success can be achieved are obscure. As the nature of work changes, it looks less and less like labour and more like a form of leisure, while leisure itself is chameleon-hued and without standards as to what is approved or what is meaningful.

The younger generations protest by their own peculiar methods. Since there is nothing positive to revolt against, they adopt an evasive nihilism. The older generations meanwhile, try to look as if they are busy, or at least amused. But what can profitably engage or delight them has been sanctioned neither by nature, religion or tradition. Therefore they seek to identify themselves with some group. The group itself does not know where it is going, or why; and the individual is thus put in the position of wanting to adjust himself to something which is itself unsure and changing.

Conformity is the most obvious enemy of the freedom of free time. Other enemies are forces which have their origin in technology and in urbanism. When we speak of the machine as a corrupter and belittler of humanity, we must recognize that it has its clear effects upon man.

The machine sets its own rhythms, exacts its own standards and style; to derive its full advantages is necessarily to yield in some measure to its subtle compulsions. The leisure which results from its efficiency will be a different leisure from that which emerged from a culture based on agriculture or handicrafts. The clock will dominate it; a certain mechanistic quality will colour its enjoyments.

The machine says, in effect, to modern man: "I will give you an unprecedented degree of freedom from regular work; but you can have this only if you employ your new leisure in making use of my output." In accepting the gift of free time, modern man accepts also the challenge to occupy this time consuming the machine's progeny. The result is a leisure necessarily active, involving men and women in the purchase and use of all kinds of equipment and gadgetry. It is a leisure in which passive contemplation or idle enjoyment of nature seems to have in it a touch of oddness and even infidelity.

In much the same way, modern leisure is the child of urbanism. Only the great city could provide the market for mass-produced goods. The instancy of communication within it, the rapid spread of each latest fashion or fad, creates a public ready to absorb and to discard in an accelerating rhythm.

The individual may attempt to set his own pace, enjoying in some rural retreat the time which the city did so much to create, but the city exacts its revenge. Its standards pursue the fugitive. The further reaches of the countryside — to say nothing of suburbia or exurbia — still echo the urban note. And the pace of the city is continuous. Machine-like, it keeps going at all hours of the day and night, and to attain maximum efficiency runs without account of the human routine. People take their time off without the sanction of nature and contrive their amusements according to the latest dicta of the merchandisers.

The clock, the gadget and the crowd — these three give to modern leisure much of its particular tone and quality. I am tempted to add a fourth: the child — or, more accurately, the children. Family life is no longer the creator of free time, as it was in simpler societies where a numerous offspring provided hands for the harvest and security in old age.

But the family to a remarkable extent has become the object to which free time is devoted. The shorter working hours, the weekends, the vacations, have all become occasions for family rituals, from washing the baby to piling into the car for a cross-continental tour.

This return to a preoccupation with the family might have provided a healthy counterweight to the mechanistic and materialistic aspects of modern leisure. It could have restored to free time a natural organic quality, a sense of live textures and slow growth, a feeling for associations nurtured from within. Unfortunately, these results have been blurred by the fact that the family itself is undergoing a rapid change in its relationships and in the forms of its mutual dependencies.

Parental authority is breaking down; the older doctrines of child-rearing, based largely on instinctive wisdom and folk remedies, are giving way to oversimplified and imperfectly understood dogmas of Freud. The children are withdrawing from parents who seem to have surrendered their former role as authoritative guides and are rebelling against a society which seems to offer them no relevant goals.

On the material side, meanwhile, the disappearance of the servant class has left the household in disarray.

Leisure spent in the family circle is thus not likely to be any less tense or nerve-ridden than the time spent in the mêlée of the social order itself.

The question "How free is free time" must therefore be answered in a qualified way. Commitments, pressures and conformities make the hours spent away from the job less than free; the subjection of the modern citizen is to something else than work. It is important, however, that in despair or confusion he should not deliberately turn away from freedom, denying it and seeking to escape its burden.

Much of what may be called "unfree time" — time away from the job but bartered to compulsion or necessity — is the result of the desire to escape leisure. The "second job" and many civic or charitable activities, like exhausting rounds of social engagements, are less a way of spending leisure than a way of avoiding it. Within the work process, routines and habits seem to be carried forward with the subconscious urge to make work consume a larger part of life and thus to reduce the threat of having to decide for oneself what to do.

Much of today's red tape and all-encompassing paperwork is subtle evidence of the same drive that makes the worker indulge in feather-bedding and other delaying tactics. It is dangerous to generalise in this area, where motives are varied; but surely the general compulsion to buy derives in part from a desire to put oneself in bondage to the instalment plan and thence to overtime or a second job.

At the very least it can be said that people who really valued leisure would be less apt to encumber themselves with purchases which keep their nose so assiduously to the grindstone.

To accept time as a boon is the beginning of the power to organise and manage it. The wise individual can then decide how to give it content and form. Some of the hours which might otherwise be free he may deliberately choose to forfeit to some regular, obligatory tasks, in effect accepting the concept of two jobs, one paid and one unpaid. Other stretches of time he may keep wholly unplanned. The larger amount of disposable time falls between the obligated and the wholly free — hours in which the individual accepts repetition, pattern and routine, yet keeps the sense of being able to move at his own pace, to stop when he feels ready, and to set himself moderate and attainable goals.

Efforts by polls and other inquiries to distinguish leisure from non-leisure activities invariably come up against the dead end of subjectivity. What is pure pleasure for one man is work for his neighbour, or what is pleasure in some circumstances is not so in another. A man may play golf for the sake of the game or because it is a way of making a business deal; one will genuinely enjoy participation in civic affairs, another will look upon it as a bore undertaken only because the community or his corporation expects it of him. But the very fact that the line between leisure and non-leisure is drawn subjectively gives us a clue as to how time may be given meaning. The sociologist's despair may be the saving of the individual, for it becomes plain that we can ourselves determine within a wide range whether or not our time shall be genuinely free, whether it will be enjoyable or merely burdensome.

Take cooking, for example. It is the most inescapable of housewifely chores. It was once unquestionably accepted as woman's work, with the attitude that nothing could be done about it. But the new emphasis on leisure has affected the kitchen, making it less burdensome and cheerless, bringing into it recipes and ingredients from all parts of the world. For the housewife who wants to make it so, cooking can be both easier and more exotic than any other period; nor is the husband immune from being lured to try its art.

Similarly, the new shopping centres can have the effect of making marketing once again, as it has been in the past, something akin to going to a fair. The tendency to bring the whole family, and to shop at hours ordinarily given for recreation, is obviously part of a new pattern. The whole do-it-yourself movement has been of ambiguous implication; for it is in part, surely, a necessity imposed by the decline of personal service. But it can also become, for the man who has some skill with tools and has pride in his own possessions, a leisurely and enjoyable way of passing the time.

Civic affairs seem in many ways to enter most bewilderingly into the leisure pattern. Work for the community should in one sense be the first end of leisure. The Greeks conceived of the citizen as essentially the man who was not bound by work; in eighteenth century England the land was governed by the aristocratic leisure classes. Yet for those Americans who today carry on the voluntary associations in which the national life is so rich, involvement is often a pure chore, either imposed by pressures from without or by a sense of stern duty from within. Modern leisure in general has been accompanied by a marked return to individual, as opposed to common enjoyments. Having taken on possessions and made the home a centre of gadgetry, the citizen finds that public activities draw him away from the true centre of his life.

Yet these activities can — and if democracy is to be vital they must — be a part of the substance of leisure. When they become professionalized and a matter of routine work, they lose a significant quality. When they are mere chores they lose something also. By observing certain rules in regard to civic undertakings it is possible, I believe, to keep them truly voluntary and truly leisurely.

Thus various activities can be infused with the quality of leisure. No less important, the expanse of time can be reapportioned and redivided. If all our vacations came in the form of one long sabbatical; or if all the hours devoted to cooking or shopping in a lifetime were imposed upon the housewife in one unbroken period, time would have a different substance from what it possesses when vacation or cooking or shopping come at decent intervals and in reasonable bulk. We accept certain patterns of time-allocation, without asking whether they are the most varied and fruitful.

The whole question of vacations must be reviewed in the light of people's changing habits and preferences, as well as in the light of what we know about the effects of time. Does a month bring more rewards than two periods of a fortnight each, summer and winter? In what circumstances and for what groups in the population is the longer vacation, comparable to the academic "sabbatical," to be encouraged? Within limits these choices are left open to individuals and then a wide range of options and calculations come into play.

What is true of vacations is true to an even greater extent of the life cycle as a whole. Is our present way of grouping time off, with the large bulks of it at the beginning and the end of the life span, necessarily the best? An older friend of mine used to claim that he had been much and happily idle in youth, when it was a joy to him to wander in the woods and be at home with nature, while in his 40s and 50s he was quite satisfied to turn to the daily routine of toil.

My own inclination would be to say that in the United States today we delay too long the entrance of young people into the working force, and then retire them too precipitously in their 60s. A mixture of work and leisure at both the extremes would seem more healthful. To accomplish this we would need reforms in the educational system. A training in youth more bent to practical ends would be combined with a chance in mid-career to return to liberal and humane studies. Actually a tendency in this direction is discernible, and it may well be the genius of a leisure society to evolve in this way.

# THE OTHER ECONOMY: THE POSSIBILITIES OF WORK BEYOND EMPLOYMENT

*Denis Pym*

*Paper delivered in London in 1981. The author, an Australian in his early 50s, was a professor at the London Business School and managed a small flock of sheep in Suffolk.*

The nonsense of employment as the framework for all work is everywhere to behold, not just in the numbers who are unemployed, but more particularly in what goes for work among the millions who are still employed. Yet we remain prisoners of employment. Our perceptions of the Other Economy, its scope and meaning, are blurred by the continuing personal and public commitments to the industrial establishment and its institutions. As employees, too many of us continue to equate legitimate wealth creating activities with the institutions of employment and sit around on our backsides waiting for government and employers to provide those activities. Privately and personally some act differently and still more hold divergent viewpoints but the problem of legitimacy remains for any wealth creating activity outside employment. The Other Economy is a domain for the adventurer but a threat to the dependent bureaucrat in us all.

It is convenient for economists to dismiss this other realm of economic activity as unimportant, derivative or illegal, not the least because it is not easily amenable to examination and measurement by their tools of trade. But economic activity was an integral part of social life before the emergence of the industrial system as we know it and we, its agents, outlawed or discounted the home and community as creators of wealth. Whereas the Other Economy possesses primary features, which would allow us to call it the traditional economy, (as well as derivative aspects), *the formal economy is the derivative system.* Its beginning as mill or factory were for machines not people.

My interests in the Other Economy come from the alienating effects of employment on the human condition and its failure to provide meaningful work for all who want such work. However, public interest in the Other Economy begins and often ends with its derivative aspects — the Black Economy. The scale of theft of time, money, raw materials, products, information, tools and machines from the institutions of employment has rightly become a subject of concern, not the least because of the damages these losses inflict on the operation of industrial institutions. But such losses find their way by many routes into our communities and homes and are thus gains to society at large. There is an element of justice inherent in the existence of the Black Economy since one of its effects is towards balancing the detrimental impact of large-scale modern employment on community life.

Whereas the formal economy represents an attempt to set economic activity apart from the rest of life and to establish the authority of contrived, less natural modes of human conduct, the Other Economy is inextricably intertwined with community life and, far from being an enemy of the community, is fundamental to its health.

The equating of the Other Economy with the Black Economy is but one illustration of how constrained we are by a perceptual frame which limits the possibilities of economic life beyond employment. For this under-institutionalized domain, as Berger (1973) describes it, all formal education is a training to incapacity. Not surprisingly those who are least involved in it and most fearful of its potentialities are the educated, professional, employed, middle-classes. Visual literary man is no more at home in the Other Economy than he is in his own.

Unfortunately, some of his more puny efforts to document the Other Economy make use of the "facts and figures" provided by the institutions of the industrial establishment. Attempts to explore the Other Economy through this discrepant "information" only serve to legitimize the existing prescriptions of an invisible domain which, beyond our own imaginations, ought only to be circumscribed by questions of morality and community interest.

I am not arguing for the replacement of the formal economy by the Other. Clearly we need both. We need a dual economy with one aspect highly mechanized and automated and the other for people, creating wealth on a human scale. The case for the Other Economy is both economic and social. Man needs work. He needs to rebuild his communities. He needs the chance to be free from the debilitating effects of continuing subjection by machine in the formal economy where he is needed less and less. The primary purpose of employment is no longer economic but social control and it represents a very expensive, wasteful device for exercising controls which are in the main unnecessary. The legitimisation and pursuit of tasks, projects and economic activities in general outside the bounds of the institutions of employment provide the way out of our current economic insanities.

### The Other Economy as a Social System

The Other Economy embraces those discounted and largely ignored aspects of wealth created by people in the community. However, this community does not spring from local government, parish council, school, church and voluntary organisations so much as those vague, fluid networks of relations between people based on a mass of commonplace, taken-for-granted, everyday activities, many as routines, some spontaneous, in which we all engage in varying degrees. The most profound and powerful aspect of the Other Economy is its invisibility, which constitutes no problem for the insider but explains"why many educated, professional, industrial men are likely to write it off as under-institutionalised and therefore of minor consequence.

Which is, of course, to miss its raison d'être for the Other Economy depends on organisation not organisations and an implicit understanding and acceptance of convivial relations as the real basis of social order. The human brain not the computer is its memory store. In Britain today, those institutions which nurture convivial relations are the home, pub, club and cafe. People who seek to improve our lives should not ignore their enormous relevance in tackling the social and economic issues we now face.

Though we are not all employed, we are *all* party to a million activities, some pursued in isolation, others jointly, which, employment notwithstanding, make up the greater proportion of the total wealth created by man's *own* efforts. The Other Economy begins at home where more than a third of all capital is invested and each of us spends more than half of our waking lives. In this private, highly personalised world we make, repair and grow an unimaginable number of things — the bulk of which have no price on them unless we value them specifically as economic activities. Such discounted wealth is produced without written rules and procedures, formal instruction, police or government, but by people acting responsibly. There can be no more sophisticated, remarkable organisation nor one that works better than the set of arrangements woven around our domestic lives which are based on our experiences of life but, from the vantage point of our industrial institutions, might have come from nowhere. The superiority of this organisation owes much to routines, rites, norms and values which derive from, and hold fairly close to, human nature.

For an ever increasing number of people, these domestic arrangements are also central to their lives — housewives, the self-employed working from home, retired folk, the unemployed and refugees from school. Such diverse parties inevitably have widely differing attitudes to their circumstances.

From those for whom home is like a prison — the reluctant housewife and the unemployed bread-earner — to those who view their domestic life as the spring-board to adventure and the chance to exercise maximum control over their own lives. Every sphere of activity has its advantages and disadvantages and in the quest for work in the Other Economy we must for the present discount and ignore many of the problems. Justification for doing so is the extent to which the negative experiences of life outside employment are a consequence of employment itself.

The kinds of factors which determine the vitality of community include:- the amount of time its members spend in it, the extent to which their activities involve them in joint action, the proportion of its members whose social and economic interests are interwoven, the prevalence of people working from their homes and the like. Another sign of vitality is the growing force of dissident community groups who recognise the inability of industrial institutions to put things right and take matters into their own hands; squatters occupying empty houses; vigilantes who patrol the streets of big cities; mothers who police the heavy traffic around schools; people who build their own recreational facilities or restore the artefacts of the past.

But for the advent of the modern industrial state and bureaucratized welfare such actions would be commonplace and not associated in any way with dissent. However, these developments are dangerous for they teach us that when two or more people are doing some task together they are contributing to social order. It is not powerful central government, rules and regulations and a disciplined police force presiding over a mass of unrelating people who exist in solitary confinement in identical boxes which makes for the better life, but people doing things together for themselves and each other. Disquieting as the recent riots in major British cities (summer 1981) may have been, to the extent that they involved joint action against the values and agents of the industrial establishment, they were also signs of the revival of community.

However, a vital, influential, Other Economy is one that doesn't just react to the excesses and failings of the Formal System but possesses its own self-sustaining energy. The backbone of the Other Economy as a social system are its small businesses and the self-employed whose unheralded activities do so much to sustain real community.

These are the very businesses the industrial establishment variously dismisses as "inefficient," "in need of capital" or "ripe for take-over." It is their contribution to a variety of social as well as economic needs which ought to free them from paying taxes to central government.

In my experiences the Other Economy in England is essentially person-based unlike its counterpart in Italy where the family provides the hub of activities or perhaps Northern Spain where collectivist activities might provide the focus. This is not to deny the scope for co-operative, commune and the extended family in the Other Economy but to acknowledge the powerful influence of individualism in the private world of the English, in contrast to the public world where individualism is paid much lip service. Any examination of the Other Economy in England must begin with the person.

In contrast with the lethargic attitudes to work shown by many people in employment, the self-employed exhibit plenty of energy and enthusiasm and number among the few who have an optimistic view of our economic and social futures. There are several reasons for this. Firstly, the question of ownership. In contrast with his employed brother, the self-employed person owns his own skills, products, time and space — until he begins to employ others. This means that he is in large measure able to structure his existence around the demands of his task and his own needs.

In contrast with the industrial cultures where taste is widely denigrated, he makes much of his primary economic activity. For example, he exhibits some reluctance to exchange his products and skills, which he sees as part of himself, merely for money which meets his economic needs but does little to sustain his style of life. He often prefers to barter and exchange his products and skills among friends and associates because these activities provide the basis of more lasting and meaningful relations. The self-employed person frequently has quite definite views about the kinds of people for whom he will work and are worthy of the products of his labour.

Reciprocity, the balance between giving and receiving behaviour, matters to him. By contrast, in the bureaucratised relationships of modern employment it is not unusual to find the task being ignored and roles fixed around giving (expert, teacher, professional, bureaucrat) or receiving (delinquent, sick, old, learner) so that the notion of balance gives way to expert arrogance and the receiver's loss of dignity and self-respect. Having real skills and tasks and being able to use these in transactions is important to people for whom the Other Economy is at the centre of their lives. The importance of task and the need for convivial relations around that task is also borne out by the reluctance of those operating in the Other Economy to travel great distances (shades of the territorial imperative). Living well is valued more highly than accumulating wealth and the emphasis on trade in the formal economy is replaced by an emphasis on self-sufficiency.

The notion of economic self-sufficiency has become something of a romantic fad associated with middle-class trendies and drop outs. However, the egotistical quest of elements of the middle-classes for some romantic past are soon modified by experience as they discover the range of items, skills and services they do not possess. Their discoveries either drive them out of their fantasy worlds or into pub, club or cafe in search of the people who possess what they don't have and so into some kind of understanding of the link between self-sufficiency and community.

Another dimension of social order based on conviviality is trust. It goes with notions of equity, fairness and reciprocity among those who are part of the same community. In a world in which people eschew paperwork and industrial institutions like the plague, the bureaucratic mind is struck by the casual manner in which economic transactions are frequently conducted. The recipient of goods or services is often left "to put it right" in terms of values and equivalents in his own time. Underlying this casualness is recognition that the contravention of trust spells the end of a relationship. Few can afford such consequences in a relatively small community. Crude reference is made to market values and equivalents in establishing worth or price. Cash payments for work rendered show much more stability and are less influenced by inflation than similar transactions within or with the world of employment.

The morality which guides relationships between people in the same community does not necessarily hold with outsiders, a fact which signals the need for a central authority, if somewhat diminished. It would be naive to claim that industrial institutions have little influence on the workings of the Other Economy but those who live within the community often behave in ways which suggest it does not exist. Relations with industrial institutions are kept to a minimum and seldom discussed. Occasionally, where paths do cross to the disadvantage of the self-employer or do-it-yourselfer, intense verbal hostility is expressed but the actions which follow are precipitated by the injured party and his friends, quietly, effectively and usually by night. In the Other Economy notions of justice hold closer to laws of nature than those of industrial institutions. It is important to recognise the differences between the meaning and place of "the law" in the formal and informal systems. Industrial man is a rule-follower adhering, like a machine, to rules set from without. The convivial society has man as rule-maker, shaping and fashioning appropriate behaviour for his circumstance — a far nobler task for man.

The description above suggests the kind of parties likely to find advantage in the Other Economy. Undoubtedly, those who possess manual skills with domestic applications and don't depend heavily on expensive machinery have enormous opportunities. Similarly locals and those who spend most of their time in the community are more likely to gain access to its networks — permanent residents, older people, people who are prepared to frequent pub, club and cafe and visit the homes of others. Such people have a broad-based knowledge of the goods and services available and in terms of advising newcomers are often aware of the nature and extent of local shortages and needs. Women, who are not home-bound by children, are well placed to make the best use of the Other Economy unless they choose the employment way. Yet some people who meet most of these criteria are still unable to gain acceptance in these local networks because their mannerisms, conduct or use of language suggests superiority and pretence, allied with a phoniness which turns others away. Contrived modes of behaviour seldom survive the loss of their institutional basis.

The real superiority of the Other Economy, from this observer's viewpoint, lies in the style of life it offers. Apart from its economic and social opportunities there is scope for personal development which is difficult to find within the institutions of industrial society. Personal development, not to be confused with socializing into roles, has two prerequisites. One is the availability of meaningful tasks through which to relate to others and establish notions of excellence, and the other is example.

Formal education and the mass media have done much to demolish the 'idol' or 'hero' as a basis for emulation and ultimately, divergence. But people in both economies still recognise excellence in others when asked to identify work colleagues whose efforts and judgement they value. This local "hero" to whom we attribute excellence is not in other ways very visible to us but he has magical proportions. His competence is typically in making connections. In a period of abundance and institutional commitment to growth, those who fix, connect and maintain have little public value. There is not much scope for "the fixer" when our commitment to production offers cheap replacement whether of people or machines. But the re-emergence of scarcity and the ecological frame are already challenging the production ethos even within employment. In a way of life dominated by contrived conduct, the fixer is driven to the margins of society and into the Other Economy where, as a person who prefers to define time and space his way, he finds more opportunity to pursue his own preoccupations. His particular competence is less the result of schooling than the outcome of experiences he has sought out for himself. His superior perception of reality comes from his marginality and an ability to re-connect the compartmentalized experiences imposed upon us by industrial institutions. His credit is our private, but not yet public, acknowledgement.

Our man tends to be self-employed or acknowledged for his independent position within employment. He may be the self-employed professional holding closely to the ideals of professionalism — excellence, service and autonomy; the fashioner of useful objects from waste; the conservationist who not only preserves, but breathes new life into the old which is of value; the social bonder and, as handyman, the repairer of machines, tools, clothing and a thousand household artefacts. Above all he is the embodiment of resourcefulness. He possesses what we know we have lost. Finally, let us give him a label that does not seek to capture and unravel his magic, but might allow him to emerge as a model, convivial hero. Let us call him the bricoleur.*

## Work in the Other Economy

Over the past half century vast capital expenditure on the home and its contents have added to the wealth-creating potential of the domestic economy. Perhaps the greatest fillip central authorities could give to the realisation of that potential would be through the payment of a minimum wage to every adult citizen, sufficient to free a large number of our forefathers who built the modern industrial system.

As well as boosting do-it-yourself activities a minimum income would lead in the first instance to the discovery on a wide front of those substantial work opportunities that already exist in the Other Economy in the maintenance and servicing of home buildings, machinery and equipment. In the 1980s money lenders are showing an unprecedented interest in home and personal loans and not without reason.

## Towards Community Maintenance

There are some signs of a decline in the production/consumption ethic and certainly, with the re-emergence of interest in conservation and maintenance, that we could quickly and easily adopt a more ecological approach to living in our private worlds. The threat of finite resources; the escalating costs of raw materials; the loss of quality on every front; reassessments of the value of "the out-dated" which implies some questioning of psychological obsolescence; all these and more are characteristic of this changing outlook.

*This description is highly sexist. Women are more familiar with this mode of being than men, and a million housewives come close to this heroic image.

This coincides with the breakdown of collusive relationships within the industrial establishment which once concealed the true costs of large-scale organisation. In addition our industrial institutions are not able to shift their efforts from production to maintenance very easily because, even if they wanted to, their after sales and repair services are not on a cost par with their production operations. So what happens when wayward customers decide to make their "old" cars, washing machines, cookers, televisions, and an endless list of electrical appliances and kitchen equipment go on "for a few more years"? Why, confronted with the high costs of institutional maintenance, they turn, as they are doing now, to self-employed operators with an affinity for their particular machines and equipment, access to spares frequently cannibalized from old models, who are able to provide a personalized service, cheaper.

Much the same process is taking place with housing itself. Raw material costs, shortages of building land, mountains of building regulations and the political and social difficulties associated with mass building programmes are making life difficult for building firms but of course, providing a field day for self-employed bricklayers, plumbers, joiners, plasterers and countless handymen who can renovate, extend and repair existing housing stocks. The escalating costs of energy lead many home owners to reconsider their heating and insulation arrangements so offering still more opportunities to those working from home.

In a smaller way similar opportunities are emerging in areas like transport and welfare and for the same reasons — the cost and ineffectiveness of large-scale transportation and bureaucratized welfare. Community opposition to extensions of the concrete and tarmac jungles; and to giant transport vehicles allied with the shift towards self-sufficiency provide opportunities for local, small-scale, transport services for both passengers and goods. In the welfare field, home nursing, many professional advisory services, home catering, local self-help groups and the like are springing up to fill the gaps created by shortcomings in state welfare operations.

In the above and similar fields, the employment prospects may be bleak but the work available is seemingly limitless. Few self-employed people working in them have any need to advertise their services even in the "current economic climate." But those who wish to venture into the Other Economy cannot wait for government, educators or any other authority to help them.

They have to get out and canvass their own community for opportunities, success depends more on the possession of good local knowledge than the requisite skills. While the conventional routes to skill are more (schooling) or less (apprenticeships) available, the enterprising young person may do better falling in with a self-employed person with a good reputation in his or her chosen area. He must also be prepared to forego anything but the most basic of wages for a year or two while learning the job. The time is ripe for a return to the old master-pupil relationship in which the pupil paid (via parents) for the privilege of working with his master.

Maintenance operations around the home will spread to community concerns as the shortcomings of local government services grow and we become less prepared to pay ever increasing rates. Already more and more of direct service effort is passing to contractors and sub-contractors while the number in offices pushing paper never seems to diminish. Linked with our own retreat from employment, even coinciding with it, we can expect our own increasing involvement in a host of community services — education, rubbish disposal, the maintenance of classified buildings, beautification of the environment etc.

## Misconceptions

The observer of the Other Economy is, like the writer, likely to be middle-class, so his views on its potentialities will be coloured by the opportunities it offers his class and kind. Consequently, much, perhaps too much, is made on the one hand of the chances of a return to cottage industries and of the revival of arts and crafts, and on the other hand, of the opportunities high technology, particularly electronics, offers middle-class man to transfer his privileged activities in employment to the home. The nostalgia for the past and the romantic quest for a worthy task has much to do with our need to escape from the rat race and the mindless activities in which so many technical, professional and managerial employees are now engaged.

Similarly, the electronic dream, as it is currently pursued, presupposes that these very developments which have public and financial support (e.g. computerization, the 'information revolution') have relevance for living and community beyond the maintenance of employment and its institutions. We do know that computers, mass media television systems, corporate paper duplicating devices and the like, aid centralised authorities, the extension of bureaucracy and probably add to our experiences of isolation, loneliness and alienation.

They contribute far less to collective wealth and community than we think. Electronic devices which enhance the convivial society in, for example, freeing man from the dictates of employment (automation), the telephone and new video systems which offer the user real control, are of a very different ilk.

## Community Production

Inevitably there is.scope for small scale production operations in the Other Economy, particularly in quality consumer goods — foodstuffs, clothing, furniture, household effects. Many specialist machinery and systems requirements of the formal economy, when creativity and ingenuity are required, may be produced in and around the home.

Food production seems likely to involve a large number of people, as much for community rehabilitation as for economic reasons.

This is food production that has its roots in allotment gardening rather than large-scale "factory" farming. In the run-down of large cities in Britain, inner cities are going to waste and dereliction at a faster rate than housing is consuming green fields. This derelict ground, much of it owned by the State, could be used for intensive food production as could many roof-tops, balconies and walls. There is no reason why modern cities could not rival the ancient hanging gardens of Babylon. They may have to if they are to remain habitable.

Though the opportunities for work within employment are declining rapidly, those in the Other Economy are limited only by our own imagination and the vested interests in a status quo which is crumbling fast. The nurturing of the Other Economy necessitates some loss in power of the industrial establishment — central government, employers, trade unions, the media and education. Since those who still profit most from these institutions are also their victims, the chances of events moving in the right direction are good. But let us ensure that in this transition those who are least ,able to bear its burden are not asked to pay the greatest price.

*References:*
PL Berger et al. (1973), The Homeless Mind, *Penguin Books*

*Other papers by Denis Pym:*
Employment as Bad Ritual, London Business School Journal, *Vol. 3, 1978*
Professional Mismanagement, Futures, *April, 1980*
Towards the Dual Economy, Futures, *June, 1980*
Individual Development: Problems and Possibilities, *Proceedings of International Training and Development Conference, Dublin, 1981*
Emancipation and Organisation *in* Nicholson & Wall, The Theory and Practice of Organisational Psychology, *Academic Press, 1982*

# 1. AUTONOMOUS TERRACE

A homily on the theme that in any street we could be more independent if we shared what we have. The upper floor of one house has become the library, where the whole terrace shares its books. The other roofs support solar panels for water heating. One of the back additions has become the bakehouse, another the sauna bath, and another the laundry for the whole group. The back additions have been linked by greenhouses for intensive cultivation, and the pooling of backyards has made room for chickens and a pond.

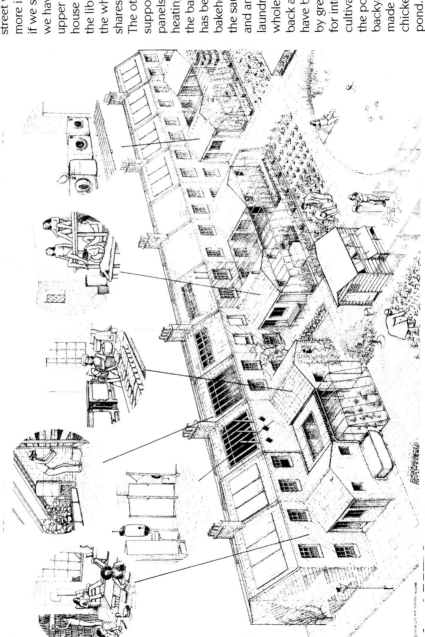

# 2. COLLECTIVISED GARDENS

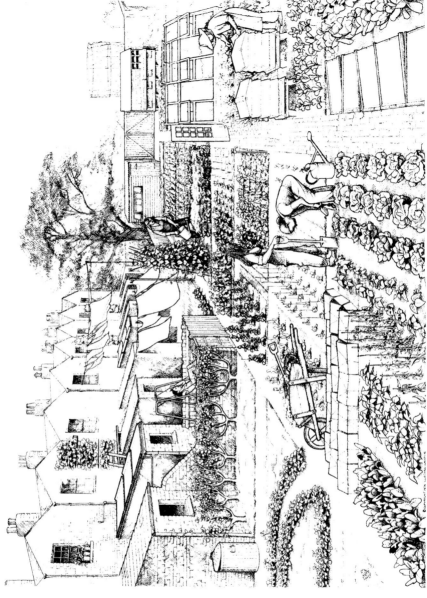

Here's a close-up of the shared backyards where the street is learning just how much of its vegetable needs it can provide. One resident is tending the compost, and another the bees. Beyond the cordon fruit trees we can see that one yard is still enclosed. Who is on that swing, idling while others work? Maybe an individualist who doesn't want to join, or perhaps it's the person who runs the creche and doesn't want the babies to crawl among the runner beans. Perhaps the artist is gently indicating that you aren't obliged to join.

# 3. HOUSEHOLD BASEMENT WORKSHOP

A group has pooled its tools and skills, thus enhancing the potential capabilities for everyone. The weaver's loom, the potter's wheel and kiln are here, as well as the equipment for shoemaking and the ordinary range of carpentry and household repair gear. The community has not forgotten the outside world: posters are being printed by silk-screen. The message is that the possibilities of do-it-yourself are greatly extended if you do it yourselves together.

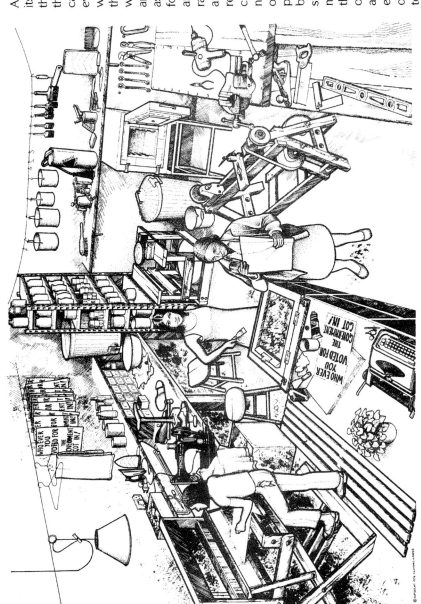

# 4. COMMUNITY HEAVY WORKSHOP

A change in scale here. In a fully-equipped engineering shop, which includes a forge, everything from car repairs to gunsmithery is going on. The Industrial Revolution brought industry out of home neighbourhoods and into the factory. Modern machinery and power tools can bring it back to a pre-industrial scale in a post-industrial society. Note than the last male chauvinist is sulking in a corner. The women have taken over the shop.

# 5. COMMUNITY MEDIA CENTRE

A former church has become the place for the arts, printing and broadcasting. A play is being performed where the altar used to be. The crypt has been transformed into a litho print shop. The vestry is now the studio for local broadcasting. In the former Lady Chapel a women's group, appropriately, is putting on a television drama. It's a reminder that the techniques of the media have been demystified. Anyone is capable of having a go.

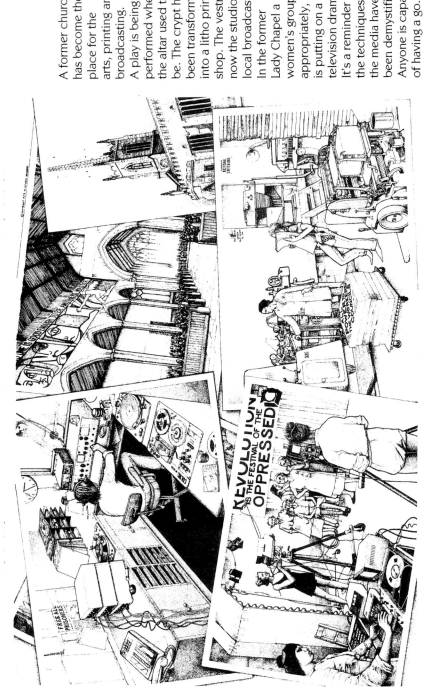

# 6. AUTONOMOUS HOUSING ESTATE

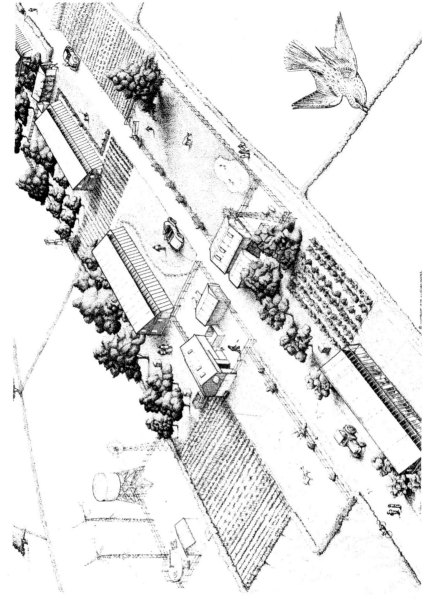

This new community is an experiment in self-servicing. It doesn't make a fetish of "self-sufficiency" but it wants to reduce its dependency on centralised services. Wind pumps raise water from the wells and wind turbines generate electricity. Solar panels reduce energy demands. Sewage is locally processed for its fertiliser potential. The estate values its fruit and vegetables. Pigs, goats, poultry and bees are in evidence. That motorist parking on the grass is yet another visitor.

# PRODUCTION: NEED VS PROFIT

## FREEDOM DEBATES, 1958-62

*All the articles in this section were published as unsigned editorials in* Freedom, *summarising a period in which the editors looked closely at issues around the nature of work and leisure. Throughout this period the Tories were in government, first under Anthony Eden and then Harold Macmillan from 1957-63.*

### Reflection on Full Employment
November 15th, 1958

The concern working people of all countries show for the question of full employment is understandable ... but spineless! Yes, spineless, because in the industrialised countries of Europe and America industry has reached a stage in its development where we should no longer be struggling to establish our right to a job but demanding access to the necessities of life as of a right: not the pittance of unemployment benefit or soup kitchens and relief when we are out of a job.

The idea that "he who does not work neither shall he eat" was an approach to life the rough justice of which could be understood at a time in history when mere survival depended on every member of the community doing their share of work. Life was the struggle for physical survival; work the symbol of life. Such is still the situation in great, and densely populated areas of the world, but not in the established industrial nations.

Yet with modifications, emulating Orwellian cynicism, the concept that only those who work are entitled to eat has been carried into present society. Production has become an end in itself, unrelated to needs. Workers operate machines which produce goods simply to keep men in employment and the machines turning. Our ingenuity is taxed to find new uses to which the machines can be put irrespective of whether what they produce is useful, harmful or useless. There are workers who spend a lifetime in the armaments industry producing weapons for their own destruction or which by the time they come off the production line are obsolete and automatically transferred to the scrap heap.

The workers themselves are the last to question the social value of work. What counts is that they have a job which provides money to buy food, shelter and a few frills to hide the emptiness of their lives. Coalminers in this country and Europe are risking their lives digging coal knowing that a part of it is then dumped in quarries because there is no outlet for it. But what does it matter to them so long as they keep their jobs. 20,000 London dockers for whom there is no work nevertheless continue to report twice a day at the docks because by doing so they are entitled to attendance pay. Even that is a job.

Millions of people are engaged in work which they despise because they are servile jobs, useless, time-wasting and from which each evening they flee at the double the moment the bell rings, but which, nevertheless, they would shudder at the thought of losing. After all everyone must have a job just as everyone must have had a mother!

Surely the time has come for a new approach to work. We are still thinking in terms of living to work when science and technology have made it more than possible to think in terms of working to live, not only for those of us in the industrialised half of the globe but for the billion human beings in the rest of the world crushed and humiliated by appalling man-maintained poverty.

"Full employment" is the slogan of wage-slaves in an unfree society. It is an insane society which is embarrassed by too many willing and skilled hands, and food and industrial surpluses. In a free society there can be no unwanted surpluses because production will be geared to needs; no unemployed because the more of us there are in the world the lighter will be our task of providing for the needs of everybody.

But one cannot legislate for the free society. It can only be born by the actions of men and women who have understood what freedom is all about and desire it more than anything else that present society. and the political word spinners have to offer by way of consolation prizes in its stead.

## More Parasites than Workers?
**November 28th, 1959**

Opening a new office block at Kew Bridge, Minister of Housing and Local Government Henry Brook said he was determined to stop the concentration of all new office employment in central London, pointing out that: "In central London, 22 million square feet of new office buildings has been completed since the war, and another nine million square feet or so is in course of erection … You can see the direct effects in traffic blocks and crowded rush-hour trains and buses."

The Minister was of course only interested in the problems created by the concentration of office employment and not in the ever-growing number of people employed in offices, at a time when office work is becoming more and more mechanised. In the United States already fewer people are employed in actual production than are employed in providing "services" of one kind or another. In Western Europe it is not quite as high though the trend is in the same direction. In Britain for instance industrial production since 1955 has appeared to be "stagnating" yet more people than ever are employed on the administrative, selling and distributive side of industry. Only last week the new president of the Advertising Association was proudly telling members at the annual dinner that advertising in this country now involves the spending of nearly £400 million [worth approx £8.45 billion in 2016] a year. "Advertising," he said, "brought countless new inventions, new products and new services to the notice of the public."

It had become recognised as an extremely important part of the process of selling and distribution, and contributed to our higher standard of living.

The contention is, presumably, that by creating mass demand for an article, industry has been enabled to mass produce it at a cost within reach of the mass public. Even assuming this to be true, it would only apply to a small proportion of advertising, a large part of which is used for the purpose of conditioning the public to choose one brand or make of a commodity in preference to others. As to contributing to higher standards of living, it is clear that the way in which the advertising industry does this is not in the *service* it provides but in the well-paid jobs it creates for many thousands of people.

The dilemma of capitalism in Western Europe and the United States is that in seeking to reduce costs of production in order to successfully compete in world markets it must introduce the latest methods of production which save both time and labour but in so doing creates unemployment conditions at home, thus reducing the purchasing power in the even more important home market.

Hence the growth of "services" during the past decade, some useful and beneficial, a large number socially useless, to absorb a part of the displaced industrial workers and to provide jobs for those just entering the labour market. Professor Ingvar Svennilson, of Stockholm University, in a study of the Western European economy in 1955 estimated that employment in services would increase by almost a third during the next 15 years. This rise, he estimated, should absorb the whole of the natural increase in the working population and also the continuing movement of labour out of agricultural employment [He was broadly accurate, services grew at a tremendous pace throughout the 1960s and '70s, and made up 68.5% of world GDP by 2014, according to World Bank figures — 78.4% in the UK].

The recent steel strike in America provides one with an excellent example of what we have called capitalism's dilemma. According to Edward Engberg, former managing editor of Business International, the two facts which "made the strike and much else in our present situation comprehensible" are:

1. That in the first half of 1959 only 1%, or 2,000 more industrial workers were required to produce one-and-a-half times the tonnage of steel that was produced in 1947;
2. That over the same period the steel companies increased their administrative-clerical-payroll by one-half, an addition of 34,000 people. To be complete the picture lacked only a similar comparison of the money spent on contractual services, such as advertising, public relations, research and development, management, market and product consultation, etc.

The issue, declares Mr Engberg in *The New Leader* (November 9th, 1959) is "not the management's right to replace men with machines but its right to displace one kind of employee, the production worker, with other kinds, chiefly salesmen and the civil servants of management."

Since 1945 in the United States the industrial labour force has increased by only 8% but it produces 40% more per hour worked. In the same period "the ranks of those who make their living from services swelled 40%, and they turn out less per hour. Machines have also, to be sure, swept many office workers out onto the job market, but not as relentlessly, and not on the floors where the thinkers and executives, now stratified into junior, middle and top, hang their hats. Executives and professionals have increased in number during the past 10 years twice as fast as the total labour force."

And Mr Engberg adds: "anyone who has witnessed the boom in office construction in New York City alone has adduced the trend for himself." Which is what we were saying in our comment on the Minister's revelation that 31 million square feet of new office buildings have been completed since the war in central London alone.

We have nowhere argued that only those workers who actually produce something are doing a socially useful job. Indeed, we have pointed out that a large number of workers engaged, for instance, in the armaments industry, are doing work which is diametrically opposed to the interests of humanity. But it is quite clear that there is a growing number of employed people who neither produce nor provide goods or services which benefit the community, who have "easy" jobs and short hours and whose relatively high wages and untaxed "perks" are dependent on the less favourable conditions and wages enjoyed by productive workers employed by the same employers. And to the extent that they accept such a situation they are parasites so far as the productive workers are concerned no less than the boss is to both of them.

Far from Mr Macmillan's summing-up of the 1959 general election result being true — that the class struggle in Britain is a dead letter — the contrary is in fact the case, with the difference today, that the producers are now in a minority! What is fantastic is they do not yet seem to have realised that if anything their position has been made that much stronger in any struggle they might engage in against the system (even though "public opinion" will be increasingly antagonistic as the disproportion between producers and non-producers increases).

To our minds workers on the production side of industry are entitled, as well as in a position, to demand either large increases in wages or drastic cuts in hours of work. Only by determined action will they halt this new phenomenon of the "service economy" as the Guardian newspaper calls it.

Mr Engberg in his New Leader article put it almost anarchistically, if we read him between the lines, when he maintained that: "As long as we persist in confusing virtue with a full day's work for a full day's pay, and until some better method than 'people's capitalism' comes along as a means to distribute the power to consume, the corporate civil servant, and Parkinson's Law, are all we have."

The "better method" will emerge, we believe, when workers become aware of their power as producers as well as of the potentialities for the full-life contained in a society based on leisure.

Material wellbeing is within the grasp of all the peoples of the world. The contribution we can make to the underdeveloped countries is not money but in the first place our surplus food and secondly what in a rational society we would consider our surplus machinery. In this way the have-not countries could provide themselves with the tractors and plant they need to increase their food- and consumer-production and the have-countries could still provide all they need and in a third of the time now spent by the majority of people earning a living.

It won't happen tomorrow, we know, but even Mr Engberg, who is no anarchist, implies that the present system is crazy and that but for it we could not only enjoy a life of plenty but, with it, plenty of leisure as well.

## Workers, Wake Up!
May 30th,1959

In coal mining, growing mechanisation where conditions lend themselves to its use is increasing both productivity and production in the industry. But increased production of coal has become a liability and not an asset.

A *Manchester Guardian* editorial (May 23rd, 1959) while welcoming Sir James Bowman's report that "productivity in the mines is increasing and that for the first time since nationalisation the Coal Board has been able to achieve a significant reduction in costs," deplores the board's decision to put off making any more decisions about pit closures for the rest of this year because "of the serious social consequences involved" and refers to this attitude as one of the penalties of being a nationalised industry. When motor manufacturers ran into severe trading difficulties two years ago, they had to work short time, "and that was that."

It may be politically expedient for the government to keep redundant miners at work in order to keep down the unemployment figures, but, asks the voice of (business) liberalism, how can the coal industry ever find its financial feet again if it is to be forced to go on paying wages for coal that nobody wants? An efficient, slightly smaller coal industry would make coal once more the strength of the whole British economy. Left as it is, the industry will become a wasting disease of national life.

We cannot see how a smaller coal industry can become "once more the strength of the whole British economy" if Mr D D Evans, Secretary of the South Wales area of the National Union of Miners had his figures right when he told delegates at its annual conference that "demand for coal is falling now at the rate of 36 million tons a year," for in a matter of five years the industry will cease to exist! But, apart from that, how fundamentally sterile are these financial arguments in the mid-twentieth century, in this age of scientific knowledge and social consciousness ...

It is not surprising that workers should see the end-product of their work as a pay packet and be uninterested in the social value of the work they do. Thus, miners protest at the closing of pits, and demand that they should be allowed to go on mining coal, even though they must know that one ton out of every ten is now being dumped. (And how much of what is sold is dissipated in inefficient fire grates, or produces the power which drives the machines which produce bombing planes, and other weapons of destruction, or useless articles and gadgets?). Yet if one is to realise the deeper meaning of "full employment," the main objective will be the *abolition* of the pay packet.

"He who does not work neither shall he eat" which is one of those slogans all workers are expected to hang over their beds is not even a truism though it seems to be widely accepted as such. In our society those whose material standards of life are the highest more often than not have never worked in their lives. But for a worker, willingness to work is not enough. If there are more willing workers than there are jobs, then what? If the worker thinks in terms of pay packets then he can even understand that such a situation may arise. But if we think of work as the means by which we produce the necessities of life, then, it seems to us, the worker's approach to the economic and social structure of society will be more positive and less accommodating than it is at present.

At the South Wales miners' conference referred to earlier, on the one hand the miners endorsed a motion urging the national executive "to oppose further closures which form part of a policy of cutting back production and manpower," while on the other, Mr Williams, acting president, "said it was no good saying there must be no more pit closures. They were inevitable. Delegates seemed to forget that there was too much coal. If there was an expanding economy, all the coal and oil would be needed, but that is not the case. 'We have to be realistic about it,' he added." (Quoted in the *Manchester Guardian*).

Yet neither the miners nor their president were in fact being realistic: the miners because their pay packet mentality prevents them from seeing the revolutionary potentialities that have been placed in their hands by the growth of science and technology, seek instead to keep their jobs by opposing their present industrial weakness to the power of the state. And the president, because instead of explaining to the miners the basis of capitalism and its indifference to human needs, like a little capitalist (or a Labour Party stooge making political capital) spouts about an "expanding economy" solving all their problems. (If suddenly the government doubled its armaments programme, and factories had to work three shifts to complete it in time, it is obvious that more coal would be required. That's an "expanding economy," with a vengeance!)

* We would agree with those readers who may object that preparing food is an art, consuming it a pleasure if both were leisurely occupations. For most people they are part of the mad scramble of life. For at least half the world's people they can be neither an art nor leisure since they haven't the means to obtain the ingredients on which to practise the art, or enjoy the pleasure.

When will the working people stop being stupid and supine? The growth of mass production and mass communications has made the capitalist class more vulnerable to attack than at any time in history. And what may have been dismissed as the utopian dreams of socialists and anarchists less than a century ago, are now in the realms of reality, thanks to technology and science. Materially, socialism or anarchism, is within the reach of the "toiling masses" … if they so wish. The problem now is to persuade them to want to be anything but contented, unthinking, pay-packet slaves.

## Wasted Manpower
December 19th,1959

Human life compared with that of a machine is real as well as being, generally, shorter. We are lucky if our life's span exceeds 4,000 weeks. Being neither machines nor mice, it takes man 1,000 weeks to learn what life is about. Of the remaining 3,000 weeks left to us (and we are being optimistic in assuming that we all live to the age of 77) most of us spend 1,000 weeks sleeping and in preparing and consuming the calories required to survive that long,* and perhaps another 250 weeks brushing our teeth, washing our faces and other parts of our anatomies, as well as undressing and dressing to go to bed or to get up.

A half of our precious 3,000 weeks gone in ensuring that the other half can be lived to the full? But not at all. For in order to provide the shelter, the calories and the soap and toothpaste to maintain life and health we must work in a job for at least a further 600 weeks and spend another 100 getting to and from that job if we live in a big city, as the majority of us do. So if we are generous with our weeks, assume that we don't have to work overtime to make ends meet and bring up children and that at 70 our pension and what's left of our physical and mental capacities make it worth living another seven years, we have 900 weeks out of a total of 3,000 which are ours to be lived to the full. Was any machine more abused, more inefficiently operated, than the human machine?

We agree that if meals are made into an art, that work is absorbing and intellectually rewarding, then our statistics fall to the ground, because we would then say that most of our waking hours are spent in a satisfying manner. But we contend that this is only possible when individuals are *in control of the jobs they do*, not only of how they do them but why. To produce coal which is used to provide a service we all require; to produce the steel, which is used to construct a ship which is needed to perform a socially useful service, these are jobs worth doing. To produce coal which is dumped, and steel which is used to produce ships which are profitable for their owners even if they only work three months in the year is an insult to mankind as well as a sheer waste of valuable raw materials.

And this brings us to another consideration. Scientists, politicians and economists are always worrying about the fate of the world in the year 2,000. One would believe in the sincerity of their concern for the generations yet unborn if they were correspondingly critical of the waste and misuse of natural resources in the present. Production has become an obsession and is in the interests not of the inhabitants of this planet, (more than half of whom do not even receive the basic necessities of life) but in keeping alive a system which, by definition, thrives on waste and inefficiency. Whole forests are cut down to produce the newsprint required for the Sunday editions of a popular American newspaper, a half of which consists of advertisements, which in turn, provide the revenue to make the journal a "paying proposition." In a non-profit society half the raw materials would be sufficient. Indeed, a quarter, for if one cut out the clap-trap and the padding as well, the editorial matter would be adequately printed in half the space. Multiply this saving by the thousands of newspapers published throughout the world today which in the main publish advertisements, and agency-supplied news, and only differ from each other on the sensational items which occupy a small part of their available space, and one realises how much human energy and raw materials could be saved. And the press is only one example. The approach today is how to exploit the raw materials of this planet and *not how to conserve them*; how to monopolise an individual's life and not how to provide more leisure so that they has more time to do what they like.

In October 1959 industrial production had increased by 9% compared with last year. Yet according to the Ministry of Labour 12,000 more families, in spite of this increased production, were having to live on the dole. We are delighted that it is now possible to produce more with fewer workers. But what is the point of increased production if the result is that fewer, and not more, workers can enjoy the fruits of this increased production? In a non-profit society not only would working hours be shortened by utilising *all* the man-power available but imagine what a saving in man-hours would result from the elimination of "competition" in industry, and by the approach that the function of a machine was not just to produce but to produce what was needed by the community. If you think we are exaggerating when we state that a three-hour working day would satisfy the needs of the community, we invite you to ask yourself:

(a) whether you honestly consider that the job you do to earn a living benefits the community; (b) if it does, could it not be done in half the time were it not for the fact that you, as an employee, see no point in working more efficiently as the boss is in business for what he can make and not to serve the interests of the community.

### Financial Crisis
July 15th, 1961

If the development of the machine, to the point where machines can be used to control machines, has any social meaning it is not that it permits the industrialist to have more power and more privileges, but that the relationship between the time needed to provide the necessities of life and the time available to each individual to live and develop, has radically changed even within the last ten years.

Yet in fact it is doubtful whether most workers spend less hours in their jobs today than they did ten years ago. What small reductions in basic working hours have been gained are swallowed up by overtime working and the ever longer hours people have to spend getting to and from their jobs. It is true that living standards have gone up and people demand more of the gadgetry of modern civilisation, and in consequence they have to work more hours, relatively, to *afford* them. But even so there is no relationship today between what a worker produces, the hours worked and what is received for that labour.

Sir Arthur Bryant, writing in the *Sunday Times* recently, reminds us not only that agriculture is this country's largest industry but that "every British farmer and farm worker produces enough food to feed 25 people." Yet it is notorious that land workers are among the lowest paid workers in the community.

We only mention this in passing as an example of the irrationality and injustice of the existing system and not because we believe that in a just society based on production for need each individual would or should demand to enjoy the full fruits of his labour. To assess the value of each man's labour in terms of money or rewards is not only virtually impossible but a waste of time in an equalitarian society in which there is no reason why the needs of all should not be met with considerably less work than at present.

The opponents of anarchism (and of socialism, for that matter) always argue that such a society cannot be achieved because everybody will want a car, a house, and this or that "luxury" and nobody will want to do the work to provide these things if there isn't somebody in authority to make them do the work. To our minds this concern with the "demands" for the material frills — as distinct from the basic needs to maintain life and health — which will pour forth in an equalitarian non-capitalist society, is based on a misunderstanding of what are the true demands that people make as distinct from the *artificial ones* that reflect the social malaise of our industrial civilisation.

An economy which is geared to satisfying needs would radically change the relationship between work and leisure in people's lives. Whereas leisure hours today represent the moments of escape from the routine of jobs and the miseries of crowded buses and trains, leisure in what, in this machine age, could be *the leisure society* would be viewed, and used, in quite other ways. Furthermore, the replacement of competition by co-operation in our working lives would at the same time deeply affect our personal relationships. "Keeping up with the Joneses," which today impels millions of people to mortgage their lives to the Hire Purchase finance companies would have no meaning in a society in which Smith is interested in being Smith and not in apeing Jones.

A talk given on the BBC Home Service in May by Mr J M Richards on the subject of *Men in Motor Cars* brilliantly illustrated some of the things we have been trying to say not only about the artificiality of public "demand" today but of the lack of realism of those who assume that such demands will be automatically transferred, with added intensity to the free society. We suspect that Mr Richards looks for initiative coming from above, when, for instance he writes: "There are … two measures that can be taken to solve the traffic problem — in so far as it is caused by the overuse of the private motorcar. One is to provide people with other outlets for their need of self-expression, which could be of many kinds. This opens up all sorts of questions concerning the dull nature of many people's jobs and the proper use of their increasing leisure ...”

Clearly jobs are dull either because the persons doing them see no point in them (that is, they cannot see any useful purpose in what they are doing) and/or because the hours they spend at work are much too long. We do not believe in trying to persuade people to make “proper use of their increasing leisure,” because only governments and nosey-parkers have the impudence to tell people what is the “proper use” to make of their leisure. What does interest us, however, is how to awaken in people a feeling of the importance of being in a position to run their own lives. For then, not only will they begin to question existing relationships and values but will develop new interests which will make demands on them for more time ... more *leisure* to do things they want to do, to observe, to study, to live!

## Redundancy and Revolution
### August 18th, 1962

“Redundancy” as applied to people is an insult to human dignity and intelligence. Only in a society where the skills, the brawn and brains of men and women are subordinated to the profit motive, where half the nation's wealth is possessed by 1% of the people, and used and developed basically in the interests of that 1%, could it be said, and be accepted as an unfortunate but understandable fact *by most people*, that “redundancy” is an inevitable aspect of the modern industrial age we live in.

And in spite of the fact that such an attitude defies all logic and common sense. But then, of course, if you try to talk common sense today you are labelled a “utopian.” To say that if our needs can now, thanks to modern methods, be supplied by half the existing labour force, it would be better to reduce the working day by half, than to have half the working population idle while the other half works a full week, seems obvious to us, but we will be told that the economy cannot afford to reduce the working week.

It can afford to have people idle; it can afford to employ them to produce nothing (such as advertising), or to waste valuable materials, plant and human skills (e.g. the armaments industry), it can afford to keep people alive, just about, or, for a minority, in luxury.

But the moment one suggests that the obvious thing we, today in the West, can well afford to do, is to spend less time working to produce what we need, and have more leisure to live and develop, some “experts” will raise their hands in horror, others with a commiserating smile will point out that only anarchists could be so naive as to believe that we could enjoy our present “high standard of living” on a 20-hour working week. We will be accused of wanting to put back the clock of material progress.

Now the implication of such criticisms is that anarchists advocate a reduction in production whereas the capitalists are always seeking to expand production. Well, a moment's reflection will show that this is not true. The capitalist "utopia" is one where demand will always exceed supply — that's a sellers' market.

We believe that the natural resources, and the means of production should be used as economically as possible and with the aim of supplying in full the needs of the people. Because it is a fact that the physical barriers which literally isolated man from man for most of his history have been broken down by the growth of modern communications, it is no longer possible to think of human needs in terms of the tribe, or the village, or the province or the nation.

Knowledge of conditions in the world around us, should make us aware, on the one hand, of the uneven distribution of natural resources and population, and on the other, conscious of the injustice of gearing national production to the satisfaction of the particular needs of a nation only. Human needs are the needs of mankind, and if we believe that all children born into this world have an equal right to the means of life then we can no longer think in terms of national frontiers and production for profit. We are obliged to think of how to harness all the natural resources to provide all mankind with the necessities of life. Today half the world starves because the other half neither utilises its natural resources to the full nor allows those who need it access to it. Professor L Dudley Stamp in *Our Undeveloped World* (London 1953) has shown that the area of the world at present cultivated could support, "if fully farmed by known best methods, at least 3 billion people on an adequate nutritional standard." And he adds:

> If the lands at present unused or inadequately used could be brought into production on the same basis, potential world population climbs to over the 10 billion mark. At the same time science is adding constantly to the sum of human knowledge, and there is every reason to expect advances which will simplify the problems of feeding the human race — if only man can overcome the barriers he himself has erected between the nations.

Today world needs are not for more motor cars, steel plants, and air lines, but for more food. Yet in almost every country of the world the acreage under cultivation is shrinking, and people are leaving the land for industry and eventually, "redundancy." Today every country should be utilising every acre of land to produce more food, and frontiers should be broken down to allow the hungry millions to settle on the uncultivated acres of the North American continent, of Russia, Argentina and Australia.

Malatesta wrote in 1920: "We must produce, say the government and the bourgeoisie. We must produce, say the reformists. We must produce, we anarchists also say. But produce for whom? And what? And for what reasons is not enough produced? Some say that we cannot make the revolution, because there is a shortage of production and we would risk dying of hunger. We say that we must make the revolution in order to produce, and in order to prevent the majority of the people from living in a state of chronic hunger."

Today we know that science plus a full utilisation of the land could ensure what Professor Stamp calls an "adequate nutritional standard" for all mankind. But to produce "we must make the revolution." But we cannot make the social revolution until enough people have experienced a revolution in their ways of thinking and acting. When workers reject "redundancy" not by demanding to remain in their jobs as before but campaigning to reduce the working week, or better still, demanding that unhealthy and dangerous industries such as coal mining should be abolished and that every man, woman and child has a right to the means of life, they will be taking the first steps in the direction of the revolution Malatesta talks about, which will ensure that production will be adequate to satisfy all human needs. The danger today is that in spite of widespread dissatisfaction and frustration among working people in the "prosperous" countries as well as in the "underdeveloped" countries the revolutionary spirit is lacking or at most is a negative one, and that before the discontent can be crystallised into a desire for action and responsibility the ruling classes will take over the initiative of solving this major contradiction of the capitalist system of production and distribution their way.

Even the Trades Union Congress (TUC) in its recent discussions with the government over the proposed National Incomes Commission has shown an unusual toughness and outspokenness which indicates that it is aware of the dangers to its own status of allowing the government to take all the initiative. For instance the TUC statement demands:

- "Social justice," by which it means a more or less drastic redistribution of wealth
- Stable prices, which it sees (with all the implications that this has for profit margins and dividends) as the chicken that comes before the egg of wage restraint
- An expanding economy.

And the general secretary, Mr Woodcock, accused Ministers of "ignorance" of what was involved in wage negotiations, and added that it was "extraordinarily difficult" to determine what was the national interest in "this very unequal society." The reason that government and union spokesmen often seem to be speaking different languages about wages is that the pavlovian reaction of most Ministers to the word would be "inflation," while a TUC man would immediately murmur "equality."

But the TUC will never make the revolution. They will seek better conditions for their members, better schemes for those dumped on the slag heaps of redundancy but never the revolution which in sweeping away the capitalist system will automatically relieve the workers from the need for the trade union hierarchy. In a word, for the union leaders revolution means redundancy and like the miners and railwaymen today, they will resist it with all their might. Obviously workers must fight to keep their jobs so long as the pay packet is the guarantee for the livelihood of themselves and their dependants. But unless at the same time, they are fighting for the abolition of the pay packet, they are condemning themselves to the insecurity of dependence on a boss who is, first and foremost, interested in making profits, and in maintaining the status quo.

## Abundance May Compel Social Justice
March 24th, 1962

In *Freedom* (March 17th, 1962), we asked the question "Can America Afford to Disarm?" and answered it in the affirmative on the assumption that such a revolutionary proposal would be matched by an equally revolutionary change in approach to the socio-economic problems of our day. We did so because it seemed clear to us that what prevented the people of the United States from enjoying the abundance which was potentially within their grasp, was the system of production based on "supply and demand" and the system of distribution which recognises only those "markets" where need is matched by the ability to pay. The failure of that system was recognised by the President of the United States himself when he confessed that fewer millions of acres of land, and industry operating well below capacity, were producing *more* than the needs of the people, yet many millions of people in the United States were living below subsistence levels. Only in a capitalist system could this loom as a large scale problem. In a rational society hours of work would be reduced to absorb the unemployed, and wage rates increased accordingly to ensure that the purchasing power of workers was at least unchanged. Thus the worker would be conscious of a real improvement in his conditions, in so far as he enjoyed the same standard of living though working fewer hours. President Kennedy seeks to alleviate the lot of unemployed millions and their families by extending the period of unemployment pay and for those whose unemployment went beyond even these limits, a system of food tickets which would at the same time relieve their hunger as well as reduce the stocks of surplus food. Somehow it seems that the kind of solutions we have outlined above do not meet with approval either from official — or from otherwise — enlightened quarters. We have been reading a paper issued by the Center for the Study of Democratic Institutions, obviously a very respectable set-up with its long list of sponsors and consultants and a board of directors headed by the Fund for the Republic Inc. We mention this because what the vice-president of the Fund, Mr W H Ferry has to say in his paper *Caught on the Horn of Plenty* is really quite revolutionary. The first point he makes is that:

> As consumers, Americans are joyously sopping up affluence, quarter after quarter sending private debt for consumer goods to record levels, and inventing new categories of services. But the lesson of abundance is even here ambiguous; for while there is enough to go around for all, not all are sharing.

"There is enough in our ever-swollen granaries so that no American need to go to bed hungry. Yet millions do, while millions of others are vaguely uneasy and feel guilty about so absurd a situation. The American farm is technology's most notorious victory. That the disaster of abundance on our farms has so far resisted solution is a portent of greater dilemmas in other areas."

He goes on to argue that not the least of America's troubles occurs over definitions.

Abundance of this self-evident variety, for example, is not the opposite of the classical idea of scarcity. And what are resources? How do you tell when a resource is scarce? Or not scarce? Are people resources? Are people without jobs or skills resources? What is prosperity? This is a particularly hard definition. The recession is said to be past. Newcomers by the millions are thronging into the stock market. The Gross National Product is at 3.4 rate. And around 5 million people are out of jobs.

Is this prosperity? What are today's definitions of work, leisure, play, affluence? Our vocabulary is tuned to yesterday's industrial revolution, not to today's scientific revolution. Abundance might, for instance, be defined as the capacity — here meaning resources, skill, capital, and potential and present production — the capacity to supply every citizen with a minimum decent life. We have the capacity, so this makes us an abundant society. Yet some 30 million Americans are living below the poverty line.

The abundance on which Mr Ferry concentrates his attention is "the disagreeable, the ironic and growing abundance of unemployment." Keynes defined technological unemployment, more than thirty years ago, as "unemployment due to our discovery of means of economising the use of labour out-running the pace at which we can find new uses for labour." Such a situation is, in Mr Ferry's view, growing every year in America as the labour force grows (1,250,000 annually) and technological progress forges ahead (permitting the discharge of 1,250,000 each year). Thus technological unemployment could grow at the rate of 2½ million without in any way affecting the productive capacity of industry and agriculture.

The question is "whether jobs can be manufactured fast enough to approach full employment, using the present definition of jobs and the means of providing them that are presently regarded as acceptable. The essential contention of this paper is that the answer is no. An apparently unavoidable condition of the Age of Abundance is increasing structural unemployment and under-employment.

"The novelty of this proposition," Mr Ferry points out, is that the majority of "victims of technological displacement will be permanently out of work." The difficulty of radical solutions based on leisure, is in part the resistance such a concept receives from "a nation committed to economic dynamism and to work, any kind of work, as a good in itself."

There are all kinds of ways of deferring the need for radical solutions. The government is spending more on "weaponry" and their action is "regarded by many as a response as much to structural unemployment as to Soviet demands about Berlin."

Then again one could return to a "state of scarcity" by "the simple act of deciding to share what we have with those who need it elsewhere in the world." Mr Ferry who is not opposed to such a plan nevertheless points out that "there might be a good deal of argument before some Americans could be persuaded that impoverished Africans or Asians have a 'just' claim on American abundance." But it is *planning* that Mr Ferry advocates, plus new ways of thinking. Thus:

- In an abundant society the problem is not an economic one of keeping the machine running regardless of what it puts out, but a political one of achieving the common good. And planning is one of its major means …
- We shall have to stop automatically regarding the unemployed as lazy, unlucky, indolent and unworthy. We shall have to find means, public or private, of paying people to do no work. This suggestion goes severely against the American grain, and it will have to be adopted slowly …
- The essential change in outlook will be to regard the new leisure — including the leisure of the liberated margin — as desirable, as a good, and to direct public policy to accepting it as a good in itself …
- Let me emphasise that I am not talking about idleness, only about what most people today regard as idleness or near to it. The revolution in economic theory that is indicated by abundance is dramatically illustrated here. Whoever heard of economic theory with poets, painters and philosophers among the premises …
- Abundance may compel social justice as conscience never has. The liberated margin will have to get "what is its due." This means developing a basis of distribution of income which is not tied to work as a measure … without the criterion of what members of the liberated margin are worth in the employment market, for there is no such market for them. The criteria of capitalism are, in fact, largely irrelevant to conditions of abundance. Efficiency, administration, progress, success, profit, competition and private gain are words of high standing in the lexicon of capitalism … a community of abundance will find less use for these ideas, and will turn instead to ideas like justice, law, government, general welfare, virtue, co-operation, and public responsibility as the touchstones of policy …
- Humanity, with its politics and pastimes and poetry and conversation, will then occupy the central place in the landscape. Management of machines for human ends, not management by them, is the true object of industrial civilisation."

Meanwhile, says Mr Ferry, "the chief necessity is to revive respect for law and government as the proper instruments of the general welfare." For without this respect "the economic future of this country … will be determined, and stultified, by the accidents of private ambition and the hope of private gain." After so much "new thinking" it is something of an anti-climax to hear that the economic revolution is to be made by a revival of respect for those two hoary old rogues "law" and "government." Like all progressive democrats Mr Ferry just cannot see that all governments whatever their intentions in the first place, must invariably defend privilege or create it if it does not exist, simply in the performance of their functions as governments. And, furthermore is Mr Ferry not himself blinkered as some of the conservative Americans he criticises, when he significantly omits to mention or discuss the possibility of abolishing money as perhaps the simplest way of dealing with the re-distribution of wealth in a society of abundance?

## Time is Life
### June 23rd, 1962

According to a report published by the Twentieth Century Fund with the title "Of Time, Work and Leisure," written by Dr Sebastion de Grazia, Professor of Political Science at Rutgers University, the idea that Americans, because of the use of machines and other labour-saving devices, have much more free time than they had a century ago, is largely mythical. It is commonly supposed that since 1850 the American working week has fallen from about 70 hours to 39, which should mean that there has been a gain of 31 hours a week in free time. In fact, says the professor this is "largely myth." The following summary of the report appeared in the Times (June 18, 1962):

> He points out that in the statistics used to estimate the average work week part-time workers are included. If figures of only full-time workers are used the work week becomes about 46 or 47 hours, which subtracts about six hours from the free time supposed to have been gained. In addition it now takes an average of 8½ hours a week for people to get to and from work, and at least one hour a week is occupied by "moonlighting," or the taking of a secondary job.
> A further five hours a week is taken up by repairs, painting and other work in and around the house, and shopping, helping with the washing up or putting things in and out of the dishwasher and other household chores are found to take up another two hours of a man's time each week.
> 'If added up,' Dr de Grazia says, 'all the elements that did not exist in the pattern of 1850 but do exist today (the machine pace of working, migration, the journey to work, moonlighting, women working) — all factors that take away from time off the job and yet are related to the job — the difference between 1850 and 1960 comes down to a few hours.'
> There is no doubting the fact that the American could have more time if he wanted it. He has what is called a large discretionary spending power, earning about $1,100

(about £393) a year more than he needs to spend on the necessities of life, so that he could if he wished make the choice for more time.

Dr de Grazia notes that it takes a Russian much longer than an American to earn a loaf of bread, but the American does not take a shorter working week because of it.

The reason why he does not, is that he has been trained to consume and 'consumption eats money, money costs work, work loses time.' Dazzled by the jugglers, Dr de Grazia says, the individual sells his time for shiny objects and while the cycle continues to spin, to hope for leisure is useless.

Contrasting the American ideas of passing free time with the ideal of leisure, Dr de Grazia says sorrowfully that "such an ideal no longer exists in the United States." He believes that the commercial spirit, in business and in government, has no interest in it unless there is spending attached to it. 'Instead, an ideal of free time, or of the good life, has taken the field. The good life consists in the people's enjoyment of whatever industry produces, advertisers sell and government orders.'

Is the pattern so different in this country or in any of the "affluent" nations?

According to Dr Grazia the average American today has, from the economic point of view, a choice between more luxuries and more leisure. The fact that he chooses the luxuries, "the good life" rather than the leisure, not only reminds us of the tremendous forces of mass communications against which we have to combat but also of the importance (in spite of its failure so far) of education in developing an insatiable curiosity in the young.

We have said this many times, but Dr Grazia's report is a reason for saying it again. People will understand and accept the anarchist argument when they feel that the day is too short for all the things they want to do. For only then will they resent every hour they spend "earning a living" doing socially useless jobs which have only meaning for their boss. Only then will they give *their* meaning to life, to freedom, to individuality, instead of mouthing meaningless slogans, and will *feel* that these values are worth fighting for. Anarchism is not the struggle for better wages, more gadgets and full-employment. It is the struggle to win the freedom to dispose of one's own time. Time is not money; time is *life*. When more people can be persuaded to think along these lines we will have taken a real step forward on the road to anarchy.

# CHANGING TIMES
## WRINKLIES AND CRUMBLIES DISCUSS PUNKS AND JOBLESSNESS

*Colin Ward*

*Colin Ward (1924-2010) was one of the most influential anarchist thinkers of the twentieth century. This essay below, written for Freedom newspaper on May 4th 1996, only partially addresses the issue at hand in this book, but in our view provides useful links to other works as well as thoughts on the declining levels of out-of-work support that have eroded people's assumptions and hopes around leisure.*

When in Grenoble I inadvertently started an inconclusive argument between two German anarchists, one of whom I had met 14 years ago at a gathering in Venice. A feature there had been the visible presence of very young German anarcho-punks (that was how they described themselves, and they were visually identifiable by dress, body ornaments and hairstyles).

I remembered them because we watched in a marquee Paul Avrich's filmed interviews with very old members of the Yiddish-speaking New York anarchist circle, and they slowly gathered that they could make out the things they were saying about a whole culture they had never heard of, once a part of international anarchism. I had also read (*Freedom* March 9th 1996) a report that at the heart of the anarchist movement in Mexico City today is JAR (Anti-authoritarian Revolutionary Youth — 80% punk, said the report) but that another group which "seeks to create the conditions for a social anarchism" accuses the JAR of "only having cultural aims — counterculture and anarcho-punk."

I've noticed that only the young belong to a truly international culture so I asked what had become of the punks of 1984, and got two different answers.

The first was the one we continually hear about the earlier 1960s generation, which says in effect that they have settled down, picked up the style of self-presentation or paper qualifications that get jobs and are struggling along at the humble end of Germany's no-longer-booming economy, but "they still listen to the music of their youth."

The second was the opposite, saying that once you've dropped out of straight society it is dreadfully hard to clamber back in, and my informant talked bitterly about drugs, alcohol, death by self-neglect and prison sentences for robbery and violence in pursuit of money once indulgent friends had lost patience.

The punk scene, he said, was not a rejection of, but the by-product of, the affluent society and once the community or the state social security system had been milked to the full, it would die out. Anarchism was not in the picture. Quite obviously my informants had passionately-held opinions, based on personal experience. They named names and case histories and I ducked out of the issue I had raised.

I have been struggling to assess the various efforts in different countries — the efforts made by unofficial bodies, with or without government assistance, to cope with the consequences of the collapse of the productive economy in the rich countries.

Being old, I remember when the young were resented because they could so easily get jobs, so I feel even more sympathetic with them now they can't. "Go to the Job Centre," say those who have never had to.

The melancholy stories of assaults on the staff of Job Centres by frustrated clients, of the fact that the staff are subject to demands for performance-related pay, and that the government is seeking to privatise them, leads to sympathy with those on both sides of the desk. Of course the jobseekers are driven to despair by the collapse of employment, and of course the centre staff have no option but to recommend clients to whatever part-time, insecure and rock-bottom job if offered in the catering, retailing or hotel trades.

It all reduced our totally fraudulent unemployment statistics, where the government had continually changed the method of counting.

And of course, the Job Centre staff are mostly separated by luck from being on the other side of the desk themselves.

The Job Centre is the modern equivalent of the Ministry of Labour Employment Exchange, an urban landmark for most of the twentieth century. I have only been inside one once in the whole of my working life, it was in the "juvenile" department and I was instantly offered half a dozen jobs.

I have always been suspicious of the "why work" doctrine preached by some anarchists, not because of any disagreement about the ultimate uselessness of most jobs, but because of their failure to notice the change in the unemployment landscape.

Fine for the clever, the resourceful and capable (especially if their parents have an income) but far less enjoyable for the young, enduring the humiliation of "signing on" if they are eligible and the continued experience of rejection.

I would relate this to known facts about not only the crime rate but the suicide rate among young males.

Consequently I have urged — both in and out of the anarchist press — that we should learn something from the economy of northern Italy, growing out of a tradition of small workshops, family enterprise and co-operation.

There are also lessons from France and Germany, where unemployment among the young is far higher than in Britain, simply because for years the British statistics have been rigged by driving the young out of the system.

Job Centres were started in France over a century ago, not as a department of government but by the unions as organs of working class solidarity. They were called Bourses du Travail, and the secretary of their national federation was the anarcho-syndicalist Fernand Pelloutier. He saw them not merely as a job information and placement bureau, but as a mutual benefit society, a haven for travelling workers and an education centre.

Many decades later, out of the same Prouhonian and mutualist approach, emerged another venture, the Union des Foyers de Jeunes Travailleurs. It has recently celebrated its 45th anniversary and insists that its task is to develop, among the people renting and seeking help, personal autonomy and the sense of belong to the community.

Since I was in Grenoble, for example, I visited a few of the mutualist housing projects and youth support network ALJI (and ate in one of its public restaurants).

It was stressed to me that "considering the way that society has alienated its young at a terrible social cost, our first task is to help young people how to be, before helping them learn how to do.

In Germany the origins of the equivalent organisations tend to be in religious bodies though, like the YMCA in Britain, they stress that it is not part of their programme to inculcate religious belief in the young people they help.

The Jugendorf Frechen is part of a national network started in 1947 by a protestant clergyman who gathered together homeless and parentless young people at the bombed railway station at Stuttgart and found them food, shelter and job training.

In Cologne the Nikolaus-Gross-Haus, named after a Catholic mineworkers' leader murdered by the Nazis, has a similar function. As visitors from England, where the Foyer movement has a continual problem of fundraising, in both France and Germany we were bowled over by the lavish (by British standards) provision and the extent to which current youth culture was taken into account.

So we misunderstood the remark of one of our hosts when he said that "in these fields Germany is about ten years behind Britain."

Thinking of the way in so much of the time of the British equivalent of these activities has to be spent on lobbying for the money to continue the work, we protested that he didn't know how bad the British situation was.

But what he meant was what he said. The logic of the market economy would mean that in the next ten years welfare provision in Germany would have fallen to the British scale. There is every sign that this will turn out to be true. I have an old contact in Cologne who for years campaigned for the homeless by setting up camp in one of the main streets. At the time of the Gulf War he set up his Wailing Wall for Peace outside the Cathedral, which carries anti-war messages from all over the world. The church and city authorities have been arguing for years about who should have the odium of evicting him.

But Walter Hermann is now under intense criticism for his support for the young jobless homeless camped nearby in the Cathedral Square, along with their dogs, in a concrete structure labelled Punkhaus.

Peace is one issue, his critics say, but punks are something else. Walter Hermann sees both as moral dilemmas facing any responsible society.

I find myself totally divided on this issue. On the one hand I am bound to sympathise with the punk rejection of capitalist values. On the other, I fear for their ability to get by in an increasingly hostile society which shows no sign at all of being influenced by alternative values.

The people from the various organisations providing rooms and seeking to find employment in a contracting market, saw the rejected young as counters in a game like snakes-and-ladders, slipping out of the real world.

So I asked one of the work-finders and they replied: "We want to grab them before they have despaired of parents, schools and work. If you find them a room and a job it would last a week and then they'd be back on the Domplatz. They'd say 'this room is a dump and this boss is an arsehole. I'm not putting up with it."

It's the psychology of rejection reflected by the rejected. It's another of those issues where I find personal sympathy for the predicament of young people at war with ideological and theoretical positions.

# BEYOND AN ECONOMY OF WORK AND SPEND

*Juliet Schor*

*Boston professor and bestselling author of* The Overworked American *Juliet Schor wrote* Beyond an Economy of Work and Spend *as a speech to students at Tilbury University in Holland. In this essay extract Schor offers a detailed breakdown of how and why the promise of progress delivering increased leisure time has repeatedly failed to materialise. A fully-referenced version of this article was published by Tilbury Press in 1997.*

In the last 50 years, as the United States, Japan, and the nations of Western Europe have gotten richer, they have become less, not more likely, to reduce hours of work.

Instead, they have channelled economic progress toward the production of more output, and hence more consumption. Among the US, the UK, France, Germany, Japan, and the Netherlands, the extent of hours reduction in 1950-1984 was lower than it was between 1870 and 1938 in every country but Germany. Similarly, the fraction of productivity growth which was been taken as leisure (or more precisely, as non-market work) has also fallen.

The puzzling aspect of the postwar history is that it was widely believed we would by now be experiencing, not a society of time-squeeze, stress, and too much hurry, but a "crisis of leisure time." In the United States, the four-day week was expected by the 1970s. A four-hour day was predicted for the 1980s. Similar expectations have reigned in Europe. The promise first of old-style mechanisation and automation, and more recently of microelectronic technologies, has been that they will liberate us from work and create copious amounts of free time.

There is a wide current of opinion which holds that this is in fact happening. The coming of the leisure society has been an article of faith for decades, widely held among social scientists, politicians, and publics. In Europe the threat of excessive leisure has become a rallying cry for those who believe longer hours of work are necessary to meet global competitive challenges. Germany's Chancellor Helmut Kohl opines that his nation has turned into "a giant theme park."

Jan Timmer, the recently-retired president of Phillips contends that employers in the Netherlands recently "drew a line," solidifying their opposition to hours reductions and the growing popularity of a four-day work week. In France, the government has opposed various schemes for early retirements and shorter weekly hours. And in the United States, the Clinton administration, despite its 1992 campaign complaint that "Americans are working harder for less," has studiously ignored the working harder part of the equation since being elected.

The major exception is Japan, where government has actively promoted shorter hours, under international pressure to reduce its trade deficits.

Why haven't hours fallen more, or nearly at all in many cases? Why are a growing number of countries experiencing rising working hours? And why does it matter? While this latter question may seem obvious to some, it is hardly addressed at all by economists, who are far more likely to focus their attention on trends in income. However, as I will argue below, an adequate amount of free time and a reasonable pace of life are necessary conditions for creating a society which meets human needs and promotes human welfare. Much of what we value about our lives — friendship, family, community, and civic society — is built on the resource of time. Indeed, time is far more important than income, whose contribution to welfare is much less substantial than is conventionally believed.

## Trends in working hours

While most industrialised countries have experienced substantial reductions in hours of work in the postwar period, these are far more modest than is commonly thought, and modest in comparison to productivity growth.

For example, Angus Maddison's figures from 1870 to 1984 show that among the United States, the United Kingdom, Germany, France, Japan and the Netherlands, only Germany and the Netherlands had more extensive hours reductions in the 1870 to 1938 period than during the postwar years 1950-84 (and the differences are not great). And perhaps more importantly, the fraction of productivity growth taken in shorter hours was considerably lower in the every country but Germany during the second period.

When one considers the far higher standards of living in the later period these trends are even more surprising. Even the Netherlands, which has among the lowest annual working hours in Western Europe, took less leisure relative to productivity growth in the pre-1950 period, when it was far poorer, than it did in the post World War II era, when its standard of living was much higher. Between 1950 and 1984 France took only 13% of its productivity dividend in shorter hours, Japan 4%, the US 20%, Germany 24%, and the Netherlands and the UK 27-28%.

Since 1984, hours of work have fallen in some countries, but surprisingly, are rising in others. According to OECD estimates of average hours actually worked per person, declines of at least 4.5% since 1983 have occurred in France, Germany, Japan and Spain. However, it should also be noted that the official Japanese figures have been the subject of debate, on account of increasing levels of unpaid overtime, which is not recorded by firms. Furthermore, the decline in Japanese hours appears to have recently been reversed, although whether this is a long term trend is impossible to say.

In other countries either virtually no change, or increases in hours have occurred. Among the countries covered by the OECD data these include Australia, Canada, Finland, New Zealand, Sweden, the UK, and the US. (I do not include the Netherlands, because the OECD figures exclude overtime working, and are not strictly comparable to the other countries.)

In detailed studies of the latter two and the Netherlands, there are in fact rather pronounced trends of rising hours. According to the most recent OECD data, which are revised to take into account the significant levels of multiple job-holding by Americans, hours of work are estimated to have begun rising in 1983, and have continued until the present.

By my own estimates, average hours of work for Americans began rising (albeit slowly) in the 1970s, but accelerated rapidly in the 1980s. If we exclude those workers who are involuntarily unemployed in part-time or part-year work, the average rise is significantly greater, on the order of 138 additional hours per year between 1969 and 1989. In the United Kingdom, hours of work have also accelerated sharply since the mid-1980s. Weekly hours for full-time workers rose from 40.2 in 1985 to 44.4 in 1995.

In the Netherlands, the evidence for rising hours comes from detailed time-budget data filled out every five years by a sample of 3,000 individuals. According to the latest time-budget data between 1980 and 1995, daily work time has increased by about 10%. Research by Pascale Peters of the VTW also identifies private sector employees as the group who have experienced the greatest increases in hours of work, a finding which is in accord with the analysis discussed below. Between 1990 and 1995, the average private sector employee experienced a rise in work time of about one hour per week.

## The economy of work and spend

The surprising pattern of work time in recent years raises an obvious question. Why have hours of work not fallen more? Why are hours rising in a growing number of countries? Why has the leisure time promised by technology not been realised? The conventional economist's answer to such a question is that employees have merely exercised their preferences for money over time. In some cases, rising wages led individuals to opt for more consumption. In others, stagnant or falling wages resulted in longer hours of work in order to maintain standards of living. In either case, the onus of explanation is upon the individual, and his or her preferences for time versus money.

While there is undoubtedly something in such an explanation, it rests on assumptions about the operation of labour markets and production which are not accurate. As a result, it misplaces the onus of responsibility for determination of working hours. Furthermore, the neoclassical approach mistakenly assumes that individuals' preferences for time and money are stable, and consistent over time. Yet the evidence suggests otherwise. The simple story that the path of the economy reflects an optimal response to stable, consistent sets of individual preferences does not stand up in the face of the evidence.

If not the neoclassical explanation, then what? As I have argued in *The Overworked American*, the key to understanding the determination of working hours is the behaviour of employers. It is they, more than employees, in whom the power to set hours of work resides.

For the most part, firms choose hours of work, attaching schedules to particular jobs, typically allowing employees only a very limited ability to vary hours within any particular job. For example, in a 1994-95 survey I conducted at a large telecommunications company in the south-eastern United States, 75% of all respondents reported that it would be either almost impossible or fairly difficult for them to reduce their hours of work in the position they currently held. (This evidence is consistent with previous studies which also show a low level of downward flexibility in hours) Furthermore, there is growing evidence that a significant fraction of US and European workers want shorter hours (see below). Thus, from the US evidence at least, the employee's freedom to vary hours within any particular job is shown to be quite limited. For various reasons, including government legislation and collective bargaining agreements, similar rigidity exists throughout much of Western Europe. "Flexibility," the signature labour market word of the 1990s, has been rather constrained on the worker's side.

Indeed, the evidence from both Europe and North America suggests that there is now a large minority of employees who say they are working more hours than they would prefer. Why is this? Where is the happy neoclassical world of "worker sovereignty," in which the market provides jobs with just the hours people want as well as significant workplace flexibility on the workers' side?

What the neoclassical approach has missed is that employers have strong interests in the number of hours their employees work. For a variety of reasons, they are not indifferent to schedules, willingly adapting to the preferences of employees, as neoclassical modelling typically implies. There are at least three reasons which lead employers to prefer "long hours" workers, and to penalise those who want short schedules. The first is that there are almost always significant per person costs associated with employment. These include hiring and training costs, payments of fringe benefits, and contributions to government social insurance programs such as disability and unemployment insurance. Because these costs almost never vary perfectly with hours worked, and in many cases are invariant to hours of work, they create a strong financial incentive for the firm to maximise hours of work and to minimise employee numbers, subject to productivity constraints.

The second reason is that with longer hours, the so-called employment rent associated with the job will be higher, and the associated cost of job loss higher. That is, the financial cost to a worker of losing his or her job will vary positively with annual hours of work. This employment rent has been shown to be a major instrument in the firm's strategy of labour control, and has a strong, determinant influence on wages, labour effort, productivity, and propensity to strike.

In the third place, firms which employ salaried workers have a further incentive to prefer longer hours: they can often be elicited without additional payment, that is, gratis. As Hilary Seo and I have shown in unpublished research from the *US Panel Survey of Income Dynamics*, merely changing from payment by the hour to payment by salary can raise an individual's annual hours of work by between 100 and 150 hours per year.

The importance of such a mechanism is supported by data from the *Time, Money and Values* survey, in which 36% of salaried employees reported that their actual hours were either more or much more than they expected when they took their current position. Finally, there are other factors which lead employers to prefer long hours: their desire to use machinery intensively and the use of hours as a signalling device to identify committed and loyal employees.

As a result of these dynamics, employers have created workplace environments in which hours of work are typically a "management prerogative," in which workaholic corporate cultures are not uncommon, and in which working long hours are often the price to be paid for job security and career success. This is more the case for jobs with career ladders, but in the United States, in hourly jobs willingness to work overtime is, typically, a condition of employment. Relatively few employees have the right to refuse overtime hours.

Thus, time spent at work, rather than merely overall performance, has become an important determinant of labour market success or survival. In my survey, more than half (53%) of all respondents report that the amount of time one works has either a tremendous or fair amount of effect on career success. And nearly two-thirds (62.5%) say that if they reduced hours in their current job it would have a negative or very negative effect on their own career success.

The predilection of employers for what I have called "long hours" jobs can help to explain the puzzle with which I began this discussion. Biased against reductions in hours of work, employers prefer to pass on productivity growth in the form of income. They do not offer comprehensive schemes for trading money for time, they typically oppose unions' demands for work time reductions, and they exact a large penalty from employees who want shorter hours. Thus, there is a structurally-biased path which I have called the "cycle of work and spend." Productivity growth is passed on in the form of income, which workers spend. Over time nations use their productivity dividends, not to dramatically reduce hours of work, but to raise the amount they produce. There is a bias in the economic system against free time.

The second phase of the cycle of work and spend is that employees take the income which they are given and spend it. Why they do this is a subject I will come to later in more detail, for now it is sufficient to say that two strong dynamics are at work. First, there is a steady escalation of consumption norms generated by rising incomes, so that even individuals who are not "consumer innovators," buying the latest products or new, improved versions, get drawn into the general rise in consumption. Because an adequate standard of living is socially defined, an individual must continually upgrade his or her consumption in order to keep up. As participants in various consumer markets know, older, unimproved versions of products lose marketability.

The second dynamic, as Tibor Scitovsky argued 20 years ago in his *The Joyless Economy* (1976), is that the positive satisfactions of discretionary consumption can be quickly dissipated. New goods, originally experienced as luxurious, and positive additions to welfare, rather rapidly assume the status of comforts, contributing to satisfaction only in the negative — their loss is painful. This creates a positive bias in spending; human beings are continually seeking new luxuries at the same time that they are unwilling to give up old ones. So the tendency to spend whatever income we have is strong.

For those familiar with the discourse of Fordism and post-Fordism, "the cycle of work and spend" can be thought of as a description of the Fordist period from the perspective of working hours. The central organising principle of Fordism is the joining of mass production with mass consumption, achieved by parsing productivity growth into real wage growth. Thus, it implies a regime of roughly stable hours. Its reverse, what I call 'inverted Fordism,' translates productivity growth into shorter hours, with relatively stable incomes.

## The dynamic inconsistency of preferences

I have put the case for my version of hours determinants rather strongly, as a polar extreme to the neoclassical view. In that model, workers determine hours. In mine, employers do the same. I raise the polar case not because I think workers have no ability to choose their hours, but because I think it is more consistent with the existing evidence. On the spectrum running from employer to employee determination of hours, I believe the real world lies closer to the former than the latter. But that is of course an empirical matter.

One type of evidence we may appeal to is what employees say about how flexible their jobs are. As I have noted above, large majorities cannot adjust their hours. A second type of evidence consists of the pattern of hours across individuals. As William Dickens and Shelley Lundberg have argued, the clustering of individuals at the 40-hour mark is not consistent with the statistical estimates of hours from a varied population. A third type of evidence comes from surveys on time and money trade-offs, which ask people whether they prefer the current configuration of hours and income, would prefer more hours and more income, or would prefer fewer hours and less income. These surveys have been conducted in both the US and Europe for decades, and give interesting insights into the determination of hours.

The evidence from surveys shows that majorities of workers, for long periods of time, have expressed relative satisfaction with their hours of work relative to pay. Relatively few would opt for the choices of more or less work. On the face of it, this would seem to support the neoclassical view. On the other hand, workers have historically tended to express stronger preferences for more free time than additional income, and have done so for decades. What is peculiar, and not supportive of the neoclassical view, is that in many cases they have not been getting that additional free time. For example, in the United States, a 1979 survey showed that only about 5% of respondents wanted to reduce current income for free time, but 85% of respondents preferred the option of trading future pay increases. Yet over the next decade, almost no employees got that outcome. Instead, they got more income (and in many cases, longer hours). Yet by the end of the 1980s, a majority were still expressing satisfaction with their current hours.

How can we explain this outcome? As the work and spend perspective suggests, workers want more free time, but don't get it. Instead, they are given more money. They spend the money, and for reasons of social norms as well as habit and comfort, they become adapted to it.

At that point, they do not want to give it up. But as far as the next increment goes, they still prefer leisure. However, when they get money instead, the same sequence repeats itself. The existence of an asymmetry in preferences for current and future income explains the paradox. Preferences adapt to the level of income and hours which employers set. Rather than getting what they want (the neoclassical story), people end up wanting what they have already gotten. I would argue that this view is more consistent with the psychological literature on adaptation, and the growing evidence from experimental economics than the standard neoclassical assumption of unchanging preferences. The evidence about preferences for future income is thus consistent with work and spend, but not the neoclassical story. (In that world, if people express preferences to give up future income for more free time, hours should fall with productivity growth. But what we see is that they have not been.)

Thus, work and spend is a story about roughly stable hours and the adaptation of preferences to maintain that level. It suggests that workers' desires for more free time are continually frustrated, but that people accommodate themselves. However, it does not stipulate infinite adaptability, as in the case of rising hours. If hours increase, particularly rapidly, increasing levels of dissatisfaction should appear. This is consistent with evidence from the 1990s, which shows that increasing numbers of workers are dissatisfied with current hours / earnings trade-offs and would prefer more free time.

European Commission surveys conducted in 1989 and again in 1994 found that in the earlier period, half of all workers were satisfied and 35% wanted more free time, while in 1994 a reversal had occurred: 35% of workers were satisfied and 47% wanted more free time. Another EEC survey shows that in Denmark and the Netherlands, a majority of workers now prefer more free time to more money (66% and 62% respectively), and that in Belgium, Portugal and Ireland preferences for free time are growing, while in Germany and France there was movement in the other direction.

In the United States, the fraction of employees working more than they want has been growing substantially since the mid-1980s, and ranges between 15-20% and a third, depending on question wording. In the *Time, Money and Values* survey, between 20 and 40% of employees said they would prefer some form of hours reductions. (The fraction rises to one-half when respondents were offered a four-day work week with a 10%, rather than a 20% reduction in pay.) And fully 69% of the sample said that they would like to work fewer hours, but "feel that they just can't afford it at this time."

This is important not only for our understanding of labour markets, but for an evaluation of the performance of the economy as a whole. If preferences are endogenous (internalised) the purported welfare superiority of the current, neoliberal path cannot be sustained. Nations are not necessarily workaholic and consumerist because that is what people want; they continue to be workaholic and consumerist because they have been this way. There may well be a lower hours, lower income path which gives people more satisfaction and higher well-being. One they would truly prefer, if they had the choice.

At the same time, the postwar history should make us sceptical of currently popular, but overblown claims that we are facing the end of work — such as those of Jeremy Rifkin, whose *End of Work* has created such a stir in the United States and Europe. Rifkin has made an oft-repeated mistake: to confuse technological potential with economic outcome. While he may be right that current technological developments make a society of minimal human labour possible, there are strong economic forces working in the other direction.

The current likelihood is not that society responds to technological change by organising less work, but ironically, by requiring more. One reason is that technological change is often accompanied by increased workplace demands and expectations. Anecdotal evidence suggests that this has been a common response to recent time-saving products such as fax machines, overnight mail, mobile phones, and email, as well as desktop publishing programs and graphics software. The existence of these products raises performance standards and expected response times.

This experience appears to be similar to what has been observed in American households over the twentieth century, where labour-saving devices did not save labour, but merely raised standards. But there are other, non-workplace related dynamics which have been important in understanding the durability of work and spend. It is to these that I now turn.

## Competitive consumption

In work and spend, the asymmetry of preferences arises because people become used to whatever level of consumption they achieve. But there is another dimension to contemporary spending behaviour. Satisfaction is determined in great measure by how well an individual's own income and consumption measures up to that of their friends, co-workers, neighbours — as well as to certain culturally prominent lifestyles (those portrayed on television and films, for example). There is good evidence that what matters to most individuals is how they keep up to these socially defined standards, more than an absolute standard of comfort or luxury or wealth.

This has a long pedigree in economics, going back to Adam Smith. In *The Wealth of Nations*, Smith argues that standards of decency are socially determined. Even a "creditable day-labourer," he notes, "would be ashamed to appear in public without a linen shirt."

Similarly, "leather shoes" had become, by Smith's time, a "necessary of life in England." Mandeville makes an even stronger claim about the social pressures to consume. Women will "half starve," he notes, in order to buy a gown. Consumption, they both recognised, is deeply social. After Smith, many of the great economists made similar points, among them J S Mill, Marx, Marshall, Pigou, and Keynes. However, a fully elaborated theory of relative consumption was only put forward by the American economist, Thorstein Veblen, in his 1899 classic. *The Theory of the Leisure Class*. Veblen argued that as society progressed, social status came to depend on two elements: conspicuous leisure and conspicuous consumption. Members of the "leisure class" secure their status through their ability to be a man of idleness; "abstention from labour is the conventional evidence of wealth and is therefore the conventional mark of social standing; and this insistence on the meritoriousness of wealth leads to a more strenuous insistence on leisure." But this wealth must be made socially visible, through public displays (or what economists today call "signalling"). Carriages, clothing, jewels, and furs, and dinner parties (whose menus were duly reported in the daily newspapers) all served this function. In Veblen's words, "wealth or power must be put in evidence, for esteem is awarded only on evidence."

Thus, consumption is chiefly important not for the intrinsic functionality of products (the usual neoclassical approach), but for its social symbolism. In Veblen's world, individuals of all classes emulate those directly above them, and so consumption patterns "trickle down" through society, from rich, to nouveaux riches, to the various layers of the middle class, to workers and eventually the poor. As income has grown, the need to "keep up" with the leisure class has become an increasingly important motivation.

By mid-century, Veblen's story of conspicuous consumption was modernised, in a widely satirised idea of "keeping up with the Joneses." The Joneses were the suburban family next door, who proudly displayed their new Chevrolet, detached single-family dwelling, household appliances, and backyard barbecue. Within economics, their theorist was James Duesenberry, the American economist best known for the "relative income" approach. Recent theoretical treatments can be found in Congleton; Rauscher, who provides an interesting dynamic perspective; and Abel and Galli who address capital goods investment. There have, however, been relatively few empirical treatments of relativity in the literature on consumption.

I believe it is fair to say that with a few prominent exceptions, economists have ignored the social dimensions of consumption. Instead, they assume that consumption is an a-social activity, and rule out interpersonal dependence of utilities. In so doing, they assume that one person's consumption does not affect another person's, nor does it affect the satisfaction received from consuming. Thus, fads, trends, fashion, snob appeal, and "keeping up" are typically ignored. Satisfaction is assumed to come from the goods themselves rather than their social context.

My contention that economics has made an error in assuming away interpersonal utility comparisons rests on more than personal prejudice — there's not much extant research, those analyses which have been done support the importance of such inter-personal effects, such as Duesenberry's own empirical tests, follow-up work by George Kosicki etc. Outside of economics, the work of Pierre Bourdieu has been of course, extremely influential. And within the consumer behaviour field, research also supports the importance of reference groups and inter-personal comparisons.

In new research I have been conducting on American data, I also find strong support for the importance of relative, or what I have termed "competitive consumption."

The *Time, Money and Values* survey was a wide-ranging investigation of work life and spending behaviour. One of my central questions was the extent to which inter-personal comparisons affects aggregate levels of consumption, and savings. Estimating savings (and consumption) functions by including not only standard variables, but also measures of an individual's social position. I have found strong positional effects. My main social variable is a measure of how a person compares financially with other members of a previously identified comparison or "reference" group. This "relative standing" variable has a large impact on how much an individual saves and spends. Moving down by one step on the comparison scale (from being as financially well off as others in the reference group one compares oneself to being worse off) leads to a reduction of $3,600 in annual savings.

The idea is that when someone has less income than the comparison group, it is necessary to spend a larger fraction to keep up with the group norm. Similarly, for those with large financial resources in comparison to their reference group, maintaining the consumption standard requires less of one's total annual income, and hence allows higher rates of saving. My research shows that this is a very large and statistically robust effect. Moving from the much better off much to the worse off results in an annual reduction of household savings of $14,364.

Of course, social aspects of consumption are affected by more than reference group comparisons among friends, relatives and co-workers (the three most important comparison groups in my survey). There are other sources of information about social consumption norms, the most widely recognised being the media.

An approach which emphasises the comparative aspects of consumption can also make sense of the last 20 years of US economic experience in a way that standard perspectives cannot. Since the late 1980s, the policy discourse in the US has polarised into two camps:

Those who believe incomes and living standards have stagnated and/or declined; and those who believe that consumption is rising significantly.

There is evidence to support the claims of both points of view. The proponents of stagnation can muster public opinion surveys to show a negative and dissatisfied mood among the population. The proponents of material progress can point to specific consumer items, as well as per capita consumption figures. However, both sides have been largely talking past each other, unable to reconcile disparate pieces of evidence.

This is in large part because neither adopts a comparative perspective on consumption. If they had, they could see that people can both have more and feel worse off. This is because satisfaction levels are determined by comparison to a standard of aspiration. And for various reasons, that standard seems to have risen dramatically in the last 15 years.

The central factor behind the rising aspirations has been the worsening of income inequality. Between 1979 and 1989 the top 1% of households increased their incomes from an average of about $280,000 a year to $525,000 and simultaneously increased their conspicuous consumption (Lexuses, Rolexes, Montblanc pens, designer outfits, art collections). In response, upper middle class consumers increasingly acquired these luxury symbols throughout the 1980s. This was made possible by the fact that their incomes also rose — the share of those in the 80-95% percentiles also increased — from 26 to 27%.

The growth in conspicuous consumption by the top 20% of households, (defined as those earning more than $72,000 a year) — had effects throughout the income distribution. This is because its standard of living is widely watched and emulated, both in everyday life and the media (television, films, magazines). It is the group which defines material success, luxury and comfort. In contrast to the worlds of Veblen and Duesenberry. where individuals tended to compare themselves only with proximate groups, today's comparative processes also include references to the top 20%. The rise in consumer standards for the top 20% provoked a general inflation of aspirations for the 80% below them. Yet at the same time, the position of the 80% worsened — they lost income relative to the top 20%. This is a process which has not only occurred in the US, but is now occurring through Europe, and the rest of the world as well. The associated consumption dynamics have not yet been as widely felt, but I suspect they will be, in due time.

One indicator of the inflation of aspirations is the amount of money that Americans say they need to "make all their dreams come true." Between 1987 and 1994 the "dream come true" as income level doubled, from $50,000 to $102,000. Furthermore, surveys showed that definitions of the good life had become much more oriented to material goods and included more luxury items, such as vacation homes, travel abroad, a swimming pool, "really" nice clothes, second cars and colour TVs, a job which paid much more than the average, and a lot of money. However, the worsening of the income distribution meant that for 80% of the population (all of whom lost in comparison to the top 20%) the inflated consumption standards were now harder to realise, because their earnings grew slowly.

This is one important reason why the expansion of middle class consumption has not been associated with feelings of satisfaction. The major elements of the American dream (home ownership, two cars, and an annual vacation) have expanded, with bigger houses, more second homes, rising automobile ownership, and more expensive holidays.

New items have entered the middle class lifestyle: a personal computer, education for the children at a private college, designer clothing, new household appliances, restaurant meals, and more purchased services. Yet this rise of consumption has been associated by growing feelings of dissatisfaction. Furthermore, households have resorted to various unsustainable strategies to maintain their lifestyles. These include longer hours of work, record levels of consumer debt and bankruptcy, and household savings rates below 5%. When we consider that the US is still the richest country in the world, the pull of competitive consumption appears strong indeed.

The relative consumption approach can also explain global trends. In the early 1970s Richard Easterlin argued that people in rich and poor countries were equally satisfied. However, as a global consumer culture has been created, the satisfaction level of poor countries has fallen relative to that of the rich. This has been an insidious aspect of globalisation: it has created an international comparison in which the vast majority of the world's population cannot help but feel dissatisfied with their access to consumer goods.

### Consumption and happiness: Does more make us better off?

The question before us is the extent to which consumption is associated with well-being. Or, as Richard Easterlin classically phrased the issue, "does money buy happiness?" On the one hand, the answer must be yes. Consumption is essential for well-being. Being well fed, clothed, and housed has an incontrovertible positive impact on human welfare. Not only for obvious, biological reasons, but also social ones. From anthropologists we know that material goods are the building blocks of culture. We construct our societies and lives around consumer objects and products, in fundamental ways. We use goods to create relationships with others, to mark rituals and life stages, to create social identities. From psychologists and consumer researchers we know that possessions are integral to our basic sense of who we are. The loss of one's possessions can be a devastating event.

To be homeless, to own nothing, is for most people a calamitous state. From sociology, political science and leisure studies we have learned to appreciate the welfare benefits of activities such as sport, travel, and civic association. From the humanities, we know that art, music and literature can lead humans to states of joy, wonder, intense happiness, and fulfilment. When thought about in these ways, there can be little doubt about the profound contributions of consumption to well-being.

Yet a straightforward view which equates consumption to well-being, a view which has been very much at the normative core of economics, is not well supported by research findings from industrialised economies in the second half of the twentieth century. Once a reasonable level of affluence is reached (and perhaps even before that point), it appears that there is very little evidence to support the view that more consumption makes people better off.

On what do I base this rather striking claim? (First, it must be acknowledged that the literature does not directly measure consumption, but uses the variable income instead. However, this is not a serious drawback, because consumption and income are rather strongly correlated in the long run.)

The first type of evidence is cross-sectional, and looks at the relationship between income and various measures of self-reported happiness, or what is typically denoted "subjective well-being" (hereafter SWB), at a point in time. This kind of evidence is available from a variety of nations. Here we find that within countries, and also across countries, income and subjective well-being are usually positively and significantly correlated. This is also true when other factors are controlled for, such as marital status, employment status, age, and race. Higher income people have higher subjective well-being, a finding one would expect both from social and a- social approaches to consumption. I say usually, because one recent study, using the *British General Health Questionnaire*, finds an inconclusive relationship between income and GHQ. It is also worth noting that with the exception of the poor and low income individuals, for whom increases in income have large effects on SWB, the measured effects are rather modest. However, this may in part be due to the correlation of income with other class variables such as education, through which SWB may be produced. None of the existing studies have been sufficiently sophisticated to rule out this possibility. Furthermore, annual measures of income are far more variable than permanent consumption, which may also weaken the correlation.

But what is perhaps most striking from the cross-sectional evidence is not how strongly income affects SWB, but how weakly. The far more important socio-economic determinants of well-being are marital status and, most importantly of all, whether or not one is employed. But, to underscore the importance of relative concerns, it turns out to matter tremendously where one is unemployed. In areas with high unemployment, the loss of one's job has a much smaller negative impact on SWB than it does in areas of low unemployment.

Why is income not more strongly correlated with happiness in the cross-section? The answer is probably because the correlation, while strong among lower-income groups, declines as one moves up the income distribution. This is likely because education tends to raise aspirations. Therefore, as one moves up the education (and income) scale, aspirational inflation occurs. Income and aspirations move together. This reduces the correlation between income and happiness, in an effect akin to the time-series findings discussed below. Similarly, there is a kind of Prisoner's Dilemma occurring on an intra-individual basis.

And what of the time-series evidence? Richard Easterlin re-phrased his famous question 20 years later, asking "Will raising the incomes of all increase the happiness of all?" The answer, apparently, is no. This conclusion is based on a range of data for the United States, nine European countries, and Japan. In the United States, happiness peaked in the 1950s and has never recovered. These aggregate time-series studies are also supported by at least one longitudinal study which followed the same Americans for almost a decade. Researchers found increases in income had no effect on happiness at all.

Thus, the evidence strongly supports the view which holds that relative, or competitive consumption comparisons are salient in individuals' utility functions: much of our satisfaction from our own consumption comes from how we measure its adequacy in light of others' consumption levels.

Because general increases in consumption do not improve our own position, they are not typically associated with increases in well-being, over the long run. It seems that there is a self- defeating character to economic growth. Indeed, there is even some evidence from developing countries which suggests that rapid economic growth reduces rather than raises well-being. Perhaps the disruptive effects of modernisation on family and community, traditional values, and established ways of life account for this finding. Alternatively, the decline in well-being may be caused by the fact that growth is typically associated with not only more consumer goods but also longer hours of work, more television watching, less sociability, and a faster pace of life.

One dimension of the SWB-income link which has not been explored in the literature is that changes in income may have asymmetric effects. While increases may not raise SWB, there are reasons to believe that declines have strong negative impacts. For the salience of losses in individuals' calculations, see the now-classic treatment by Kahneman and Tversky.

Of course, these findings are not only intelligible from a relative or competitive consumption perspective. Even from a standard, a-social approach, one can argue that increases in consumption may be only weakly related to increases in well-being, if consumption in general is subject to diminishing marginal returns. Just as a person can become satiated with particular products (a third winter coat will probably give little satisfaction, a second washing machine almost none) so too may aggregate consumption add less and less to well-being. However, it may be worth noting that economists rarely take such a possibility seriously.

The absence of a strong impact of income on well-being can also be well-explained by the capabilities and functionings approach of Amartya Sen. Sen argues persuasively that what matters to people are their functionings and capabilities, by which he means in the former case 'achievements,' and in the latter "abilities to achieve...or in the positive sense: what real opportunities you have regarding the life you may lead." If the costs of achieving certain capabilities and functionings rise with economic growth, then a relative perspective on poverty and well-being is justified. Furthermore, capabilities and functionings may themselves have a strong relative dimension. As Sen argues, "Some of the same capabilities require more real income and opulence in the form of commodity possession in a richer society than in poorer ones."

Thus, we can conclude that the economy of work and spend does not yield rising subjective well-being. Increases in income yield short term benefits, but these dissipate quickly. Over time, even very large increases in output per person, such as those experienced in postwar Europe and Japan have not led people to describe themselves as subjectively better off. Because our consumption norms and aspirations rise with our actual consumption, there is plausible evidence that we are trapped on a frustrating "hedonistic treadmill."

## Time and Happiness

If income really does not produce happiness, a number of puzzling questions arise. Perhaps most obviously, what does make for a happy life? If it is not money, why do we act as if we believed it is, devoting enormous amounts of time and energy to what Wordsworth called "getting and spending." Are we deluded? Trapped in what economists now call a 'coordination failure'? Seduced by advertising? These questions are of enormous importance for society, and by extension social scientists. If the mandate of social science (and economics) is to analyse society in order to improve it, then our strong focus on income may have been misplaced.

The simplest explanation for the failure of money and consumption to produce happiness is, in the words of Yale University political scientist Robert Lane, that "the sources of happiness lie elsewhere," in the daily pleasures of life, a good marriage, psychological disposition, the avoidance of unemployment, family and friendship. (It may also be worth noting that money is not the only surprisingly absent factor on this list. Having children contributes negatively to happiness). Indeed, as Lane argues, friendship has a particular role in the avoidance of depression, a malady which has become increasingly common in a large number of countries. Individuals who can identify at least one true friend are much less likely to become depressed than those who cannot.

Similar findings come from a University of Michigan satisfaction survey, which found that individuals rate family and socialising most highly. US surveys also reveal the importance of such factors: Americans rank spending more time with family and friends and having less stress as the two most important things that would raise their life satisfaction. Notably, having a nicer car and a bigger house or apartment were among the lowest ranked items.

What is important for our purposes about these findings is that when we look at those factors which individuals can exercise control over (friendship, family, marriage), it is clear that the most important economic resource involved in their "production" is not money, but time. So too with community, which can only be created through significant inputs of time. Time is the crucial underpinning of all social relationships, without which they deteriorate, in misunderstanding, feelings of abandonment, neglect, betrayal, and the like. Neither technology nor money are ultimately very good substitutes for time in the reproduction of human relationships.

I suppose we all know this from personal experience. Deep friendships tend to be forged in youth, when time is plentiful and money scarce.

Maintaining them throughout the busy years of child-rearing and maximal work commitments is difficult. So too can we see this point in the transitional economies of Eastern Europe: in the communist era, when opportunities for making money were limited, high levels of sociability resulted, as many evenings were spent around kitchen tables talking (and of course drinking). As the market economy rapidly transforms these countries, such sociability is reportedly declining equally rapidly.

Our growing understanding of the importance of social capital also suggests that the input of civic time has beneficial impacts on economic efficiency and the quality of social life. But the production of social capital is based, more than anything else, on free grants of time from individuals to groups. There is now a significant climate of opinion in the United States which holds that the decline in civic participation represents a serious threat to social well-being. And, while the causes of declining time spent in civic affairs are not well understood, the rise of female working hours remains a plausible candidate for explanation.

Among the nations of the industrialised world where working hours are rising (the United States, Canada, the United Kingdom, and increasingly the Netherlands), and among the highly-educated, professional time-poor groups of other nations, there are decided trends toward rising levels of stress, time-pressure and haste. Time-poverty is leading to pressure on precisely those elements of life which I have identified as constitutive of happiness and well-being: time with family, time for friendships, time for civic engagement and community.

In the United States, research conducted by Karen Greve found strong evidence that parents who work longer hours substitute spending for time with their children: using video games, films, toys and book as replacements for parental time. But the efficacy of these substitutes must be questioned. Arlie Hochschild's recently released study of a major American corporation, *The Time Bind: When Home Becomes Work and Work Becomes Work*, shows the mounting costs for children and family life as work becomes ever more demanding. Daily life becomes "Taylorised," i.e., subject to the pressures of efficiency developed by Frederick Winslow Taylor and originally applied to workplaces. Children are warehoused as their parents spend increasingly long hours on the job, and "sped up" when parents are present. Spending time with friends appears as an increasingly utopian goal. In the United States. 54% of the population reports a great deal or moderate stress in the last two weeks, and 29% say that they always feel rushed, (Robinson and Godbey 1996).

Ultimately, the most serious problem with an economy of work and spend is not, to quote one famous American philosopher, that "superfluous wealth can buy superfluities only." Nor is it that consumption cannot ensure our happiness. Rather, the problem is the suspicion that work and spend undermines precisely those things which do bring happiness; robbing us of our time, our children's childhoods, our social engagements and our friendships. In place of these true human satisfactions it offers money and consumer goods. But is it a good bargain? As we approach the twenty-first century, this question will grow ever-more persistent. Shall we opt for another half century of long hours, accelerating consumption, and an increasing pace of life, the option offered up to us by the global free market economy? Or shall we consciously choose for something different, for lives in which we pay close attention to deeper satisfactions: to time, to personal connections, to a moral and spiritual life?

# DARK SATANIC CUBICLES:
# IT'S TIME TO SMASH THE JOB CULTURE!

*Claire Wolfe*

*Wolfe is a US libertarian writer, or what would commonly be noted as right-libertarian in European circles. This 2005 article, originally published on Loompanics Unlimited, offers a trenchant critique of the rise of cubical culture and precarious white-collar work at the turn of the century, as deindustrialisation and the bad memories of the dotcom bubble began to recede. Much of her writing can be found at clairewolfe.com*

> *You load sixteen tons, and what do you get?*
> *Another day older and deeper in debt.*
> *St. Peter don't you call me, 'cause I can't go.*
> *I owe my soul to the company store.*
> *(Merle Travis, chorus of the song* Sixteen Tons, *1946)*

Back in 1955, thunder-voiced Tennessee Ernie Ford recorded that song as the B-side of a single. Soon, nobody could even remember what the A-side was. DJ's all over the country began flipping the disc — and within two months of its release *Sixteen Tons* had become the biggest single ever sold in America.

*Sixteen Tons* is a John Henry-style fable about a coal miner who's tough as nails — one fist of iron, the other of steel. He's able to do the most back-breaking job and slaughter any opponent. But even though he's been working in the mines since the day he was born, he can't get ahead.

Merle Travis wrote and recorded the song in 1946. But until Ford covered it, *Sixteen Tons* hadn't done Travis a bit of good. Far from it.

Although Travis was a patriotic Kentucky boy, the U.S. government thought any song complaining about hard work and hopeless debt was subversive. The song got Travis branded a communist sympathiser (a dangerous label in those days). A Capitol record exec who was a Chicago DJ in the late '40s remembers an FBI agent coming to the station and advising him not to play *Sixteen Tons*.

Pretty big fuss over one little song.

By 1955, when the song finally became a mega-hit, most Americans had already moved away from coal-mine type jobs. It was the era of The Man in the Gray Flannel Suit, the corporation man, the efficiency expert, and brokenhearted distress about conformity — from people who continued helplessly to commute, consume, cooperate, conform — and gobble their Milltown tranquilisers and beg doctors to treat their tension-spawned ulcers.

This was a world far, far, far from the coal mines, with a seemingly very different set of tribulations.

Yet somehow that chorus still resonated: Another day older and deeper in debt.

Beyond all the fantasy lyrics about being raised in the cane-brake by an old mama lion, *Sixteen Tons* still resonates.

We don't work for mining companies that pay in scrip redeemable only at the company store. But we work our asses off and end up with credit cards that hit us with 19.99% interest, $40 late fees, and other hidden charges so heavy it's possible — even common — to pay for years and actually owe more than you started with.

We may not do manual labour. But we work even longer hours than our fathers, pay higher taxes, depend on two salaries to keep one household together, shove our alienated children into daycare and government education camps, watch our money steadily inflate away (while the TV tells us the consumer price index is holding steady) and suffer mightily from a raft of job-related mental and physical ills.

What's changed but the details? For all our material possessions, we're in the same old cycle of working, hurting, and losing.

And even though the FBI may not pay us a visit for complaining about it, rebelling against jobs is still a threat to the powers that be.

The government doesn't have to worry about rebellion much, though. Because today we're programmed from the moment we wake up to the moment we go to bed to value jobs, big corporations — and the things jobs buy us — over the real pleasures — and real necessities — of being human.

The news says it every day:

- 130,000 jobs were created in July. Jobs = Good.
- We're losing jobs overseas. Losing jobs = Bad.
- Leading economic indicators say economic indicators (whatever the hell they may be) = Important.
- The Dow-Jones industrial average rose … The stock market = Vital.

Every day in the media, the health of the nation is measured — sometimes almost exclusively measured — in jobs and stocks, employment and corporations.

I don't mean to imply that income, production, and other such measures aren't important. They are important — in their place. In perspective. But why do we (via our media) believe these very few factors are so vitally and exclusively important when it comes to determining the economic health of our society?

We take it as a given that jobs = good, that high stocks = good, and that working harder and spending lots of money = more jobs and higher stocks.

Then we go off to jobs we mostly detest. Or jobs we enjoy, but that stress us out, take us away from our families, and turn our home hours into a frenzied burden, in which we have to struggle to do everything from entertain ourselves to making artificial quality time with kids who barely know us.

There's something wrong with this picture.

In our current economic setup, which is an evolutionary, not revolutionary, development from 250 years ago, when the Industrial Revolution got started, yes, jobs are important. But that's like saying that puke-inducing chemotherapy is important when you've got cancer. Uh, yeah. But better not to get cancer in the first place, right?

In a healthy human community, jobs are neither necessary nor desirable. Productive work is necessary — for economic, social, and even spiritual reasons. Free markets are also an amazing thing, almost magical in their ability to satisfy billions of diverse needs. Entrepreneurship? Great! But jobs — going off on a fixed schedule to perform fixed functions for somebody else day after day at a wage — aren't good for body, soul, family, or society.

Intuitively, wordlessly, people knew it in 1955. They knew it in 1946. They really knew it when Ned Ludd and friends were smashing the machines of the early Industrial Revolution (though the Luddites may not have understood exactly why they needed to do what they did).

Jobs suck. Corporate employment sucks. A life crammed into nine-to-five boxes sucks. Gray cubicles are nothing but an update on William Blake's dark satanic mills. Granted, the cubicles are more bright and airy; but they're different in degree rather than in kind from the mills of the Industrial Revolution. Both cubicles and dark mills signify working on other people's terms, for other people's goals, at other people's sufferance. Neither type of work usually results in us owning the fruits of our labours or having the satisfaction of creating something from start to finish with our own hands. Neither allows us to work at our own pace, or the pace of the seasons. Neither allows us access to our families, friends, or communities when we need them or they need us. Both isolate work from every other part of our life.

And heck, especially if you work for a big corporation, you can be confident that Ebenezer Scrooge cared more about Bob Cratchett than your employer cares about you.

The powers-that-be have feared for the last 250 years that we'd figure all that out and try to do something about it. Why else would the FBI try to suppress an obscure faux folk song? American history is full of hidden tales of private or state militias being used to smash worker rebellions and strikes. In the day of the Luddites, the British government went so far as to make industrial sabotage a capital crime.

At one point crown and parliament put more soldiers to work smashing the Luddites than it had in the field fighting Napoleon Bonaparte.

Now that's fear for you.

But today, no worry. We've made wage-slavery so much a part of our culture that it probably doesn't even occur to most people that there's something unnatural about separating work from the rest of our lives. Or about spending our entire working lives producing things in which we can often take only minimal personal pride — or no pride at all.

We're happy! We tell ourselves. We're the most prosperous! Free! Happy! people ever to live on Earth! We're longer-lived, healthier, smarter, and just generally better off than anybody, ever, at any time on planet Earth. So we go on telling ourselves as we dash off to our counselling appointments, down our Prozac, or stare into the dregs of that latest bottle of wine.

Horsefeathers! You know what we sound like, assuring ourselves of our good fortune? We sound like the mechanized voices whispering to the pre-programmed bottle babies in Aldous Huxley's *Brave New World*:

> Alpha children … work much harder than we do, because they're so frightfully clever. I'm really awfully glad I'm a Beta, because I don't work so hard. And then we are much better than the Gammas and Deltas.

To believe how happy we are we have to ignore our rising rates of drug abuse, our soaring rates of depression, our backaches, our carpal tunnel syndromes, and our chronic fatigue syndrome. We have to ignore the billions of dollars and billions of hours we spend on mood-altering pharmaceuticals, drug-abuse counselling, headache remedies, mindless escape entertainment, day-care centres, status purchases, unhealthy comfort foods, shop-a-holic sprees, and doctor's care for all our vague, non-specific physical and mental ills.

You think that's how a happy person spends his time and money? Gimme a break!

Quit listening to that little mechanical corporate-state whisper that tells you what you're supposed to consider important — that tells you jobs are supposed to be the central focus of your life. Quit listening to that voice that tells you you're happy when your entire body and soul are screaming at you that you're unhappy.

Here's something to shout to yourself: Jobs suck! Jobs are bad for you!

Shout it until you really hear yourself shouting it — then get out of the job madness, out of wage slavery, out of the grind that keeps you indebted to government, the boss, the bank, and the credit-card company.

Oh, but wait! You'll die if you don't have a job, just like a cancer patient might die without chemo. In our society, if you don't have a job, you're on the skids. You're a poor unfortunate. You're a lazy bum. You're a leech. You're a loser. And really, truly, if you don't have regular employment of some kind, you're in danger of going down life's drain.

As an individual, of course you can escape the job trap to a certain extent. As a freelance writer, I have. I still have to work for other people, but I get to do it at an organic pace. When the Sun is shining, I can often sit on the deck or go for a walk.

The man who sometimes mows my lawn has escaped somewhat. He can schedule his own day without having to ask permission or without screwing up anybody's production line. My ex-boyfriend the software engineer has escaped, too. He works out of his spare bedroom and gets to live and work in the computer dream world he most enjoys.

That's the way it was for most people, prior to the Industrial Revolution. They may have worked hard and may not have had much. As in every age, they had to put up with the savageries of rulers' power struggles, rulers' wars, and rulers' property confiscation. But generally they could move through their days as the seasons and their own needs (and the needs of their families and communities) dictated. They had a direct, personal connection to the goods they made and the services they performed.

Avon ladies, self-employed carpenters, security consultants, people who earn their living selling goods on Ebay, reflexology practitioners, swap-meet sellers, self-employed gardeners, contract loggers, drug dealers, home-knitters, psychics — today they've all made a partial, personal escape from the job trap.

But escape can be perilous. When you're self-employed, you often can't afford to provide yourself the "safety net" that comes with a job (health insurance, vacations, sick pay, unemployment insurance, etc.). And the even deeper problem is that society — that hard-to-pin-down, but vitally important abstraction — still inflicts its values and its problems even upon those of us who make our best personal efforts to escape from them.

You and I may be smart and lucky enough to create for ourselves hand-crafted employment that doesn't force us into gray cubicles, nine-to-five routine, ghastly commutes, indigestion-inducing lunches gobbled at our desks, co-workers and bosses who grate on our nerves, three-piece suits, pantyhose, and total exhaustion at the end of the day.

But you and I, the cagey self-employed, are still stuck dealing with the consequences of a system that produces neglected, ill-bred kids, frantic consumer culture, impersonal corporations, television and drug abuse as a means of numbing the pain, unhappy and unfulfilled neighbours and family members and many, many more problems that hurt us as bad as they hurt the job holders.

Is it possible, then, to create a society in which work is more personally fulfilling and fits more organically into the rest of our lives? Is it possible to create such a choice for all who want to take it?

Nearly every writer who advocates the abolition of jobs and the celebration of leisure repeats the same handful of interesting, but slightly unhelpful messages. First, they look back to hunter-gatherer societies (who work, on average, three to four hours a day) and say, If they can do it, why can't we? They fail to note that hunter gatherers, whatever their other virtues, don't invent vaccines, construct high-tech devices, or have such amenities as indoor plumbing.

Writers against jobs also talk about making work into a species of fun. That's another great trait of hunter-gatherer societies.

It's easy to have fun when you're harvesting berries or chasing deer with a group of friends. But nobody builds precision medical equipment for fun. Nor do they plunge a mile underground to "load sixteen tons of number nine coal" for amusement.

Finally, anti-job writers are big on utopian theory: society could work so well, if only, if only. Utopian proposals are inevitably lite on key details. They fail to consider how to wean ourselves away from corporate job culture without coercion. They fail to note how modern goods and services could be produced without the large, well-funded — and job-based — institutions that provide so much of modern life. (You cannot splice genes, split atoms, or build computer chips in your quaint Amish workshop.)

So the questions are:

Is it possible to have an organic, work-and-leisure culture without slipping back to subsistence-level survival?

And is it possible to have the benefits of advanced technology without having to sacrifice so much of our time, our individuality, and our sanity, to get them?

As long as government and its heavily favoured and subsidized corporations and financial markets rule our work days, the answers to these questions will never come. We can find our way to a humane work-and-leisure society only through experiment and experience. And we'll be able to make those experiments only in conjunction with (pardon my using the cliched-but-accurate expression) a paradigm shift. The current job culture, which imprisons us in the silver chains of benefits and the iron shackles of debt, looms blackly in our way.

The necessary sea-change seems far away now. Yet paradigms do shift. Institutions do fall. And often they fall just when the old paradigms seem most entrenched or the old institutions seem most immovable.

Some of the machinery of change may already be in place. For instance:

Although automation hasn't yet put us out of jobs, as it was supposed to, it still has the potential to eliminate many types of drudgery.

Although computer-based knowledge work hasn't enabled millions of us to leave the corporate world and work at home (as, again, it was supposed to), that's more a problem of corporate power psychology than of technology. Our bosses fear to let us work permanently at home; after all, we might take 20-minute coffee breaks, instead of ten! But what if, say, a fuel crisis or epidemic made it imperative for more of us to stay home to do our work? The paradigm could shift so fast our bosses would fall over.

A wide-scale attitude change could also topple the traditional job structure. And that, too, may already be happening. How many parents are looking around and saying: "This two-job crap isn't getting us anywhere?"

It's only a short leap from there to the real truth: one-job crap doesn't satisfy our real needs, either. How many of us have spent ten or 20 or 30 years buying into the jobs = good; spending = good hype only to decide to walk away from the rat maze and do something less lucrative but more gratifying?

Do you hear many people wailing with sorrow after walking away from the job world and establishing a more home-centred, family-centred, adventure-centred, spirit-centred, community-centred life? Only those few who, through bad planning or extreme bad luck, tried and didn't make it.

Until the larger job = good illusion shatters, it's certainly possible for millions of individuals to live more organic lives, without job-slavery. As more people declare their independence, more support networks rise to help them (for example, affordable health insurance for the self-employed, or health care providers opting to provide more affordable services through cash-only programs like SimpleCare).

And we can begin to consider: What types of technology let us live more independently, and what types of independence still enable us to take advantage of life-enhancing technologies while keeping ourselves out of the life-degrading job trap?

Take a job and you've sold part of yourself to a master. You've cut yourself off from the real fruits of your own efforts.

When you own your own work, you own your own life. It's a goal worthy of a lot of sacrifice. And a lot of deep thought.

In the meantime, unfortunately, anybody who cries, Jobs aren't needed! Jobs aren't healthy for adults and other living things! Is crying in the wilderness. We Elijahs and Cassandras can be counted on to be treated like fringeoid idiots. And anybody who begins to come up with a serious plan that starts cutting the underpinnings from the state-corporate power structure can expect to be treated as Public Enemy Number One and had better watch his backside.

Because like Merle Travis and Ned Ludd, he threatens the security of those who hold power over others.

# ON THE PHENOMENON OF BULLSHIT JOBS

*David Graeber*

*LSE anthropology professor and bestselling author David Graeber explored the modern phenomenon of "bullshit jobs" in Strike Magazine's Summer 2013 issue.*

In the year 1930, John Maynard Keynes predicted that technology would have advanced sufficiently by century's end that countries like Great Britain or the United States would achieve a 15-hour work week. There's every reason to believe he was right. In technological terms, we are quite capable of this. And yet it didn't happen.

Instead, technology has been marshaled, if anything, to figure out ways to make us all work more. In order to achieve this, jobs have had to be created that are, effectively, pointless. Huge swathes of people, in Europe and North America in particular, spend their entire working lives performing tasks they secretly believe do not really need to be performed. The moral and spiritual damage that comes from this situation is profound. It is a scar across our collective soul. Yet virtually no one talks about it.

Why did Keynes' promised utopia — still being eagerly awaited in the '60s — never materialise? The standard line today is that he didn't figure in the massive increase in consumerism. Given the choice between less hours and more toys and pleasures, we've collectively chosen the latter. This presents a nice morality tale, but even a moment's reflection shows it can't really be true. Yes, we have witnessed the creation of an endless variety of new jobs and industries since the '20s, but very few have anything to do with the production and distribution of sushi, iPhones, or fancy sneakers.

So what are these new jobs, precisely? A recent report comparing employment in the US between 1910 and 2000 gives us a clear picture (and I note, one pretty much exactly echoed in the UK). Over the course of the last century, the number of workers employed as domestic servants, in industry, and in the farm sector has collapsed dramatically. At the same time, "professional, managerial, clerical, sales, and service workers" tripled, growing "from one-quarter to three-quarters of total employment." In other words, productive jobs have, just as predicted, been largely automated away (even if you count industrial workers globally, including the toiling masses in India and China, such workers are still not nearly so large a percentage of the world population as they used to be).

But rather than allowing a massive reduction of working hours to free the world's population to pursue their own projects, pleasures, visions, and ideas, we have seen the ballooning not even so much of the "service" sector as of the administrative sector, up to and including the creation of whole new industries like financial services or telemarketing, or the unprecedented expansion of sectors like corporate law, academic and health administration, human resources, and public relations.

And these numbers do not even reflect on all those people whose job is to provide administrative, technical, or security support for these industries, or for that matter the whole host of ancillary industries (dog-washers, all-night pizza deliverymen) that only exist because everyone else is spending so much of their time working in all the other ones.

These are what I propose to call "bullshit jobs."

It's as if someone were out there making up pointless jobs just for the sake of keeping us all working. And here, precisely, lies the mystery. In capitalism, this is exactly what is not supposed to happen. Sure, in the old inefficient socialist states like the Soviet Union, where employment was considered both a right and a sacred duty, the system made up as many jobs as they had to (this is why in Soviet department stores it took three clerks to sell a piece of meat). But, of course, this is the very sort of problem market competition is supposed to fix. According to economic theory, at least, the last thing a profit-seeking firm is going to do is shell out money to workers they don't really need to employ. Still, somehow, it happens.

While corporations may engage in ruthless downsizing, the layoffs and speed-ups invariably fall on that class of people who are actually making, moving, fixing and maintaining things; through some strange alchemy no one can quite explain, the number of salaried paper-pushers ultimately seems to expand, and more and more employees find themselves, not unlike Soviet workers actually, working 40 or even 50 hour weeks on paper, but effectively working 15 hours just as Keynes predicted, since the rest of their time is spent organising or attending motivational seminars, updating their Facebook profiles or downloading TV box-sets.

The answer clearly isn't economic: it's moral and political. The ruling class has figured out that a happy and productive population with free time on their hands is a mortal danger (think of what started to happen when this even began to be approximated in the '60s). And, on the other hand, the feeling that work is a moral value in itself, and that anyone not willing to submit themselves to some kind of intense work discipline for most of their waking hours deserves nothing, is extraordinarily convenient for them.

Once, when contemplating the apparently endless growth of administrative responsibilities in British academic departments, I came up with one possible vision of hell. Hell is a collection of individuals who are spending the bulk of their time working on a task they don't like and are not especially good at. Say they were hired because they were excellent cabinet-makers, and then discover they are expected to spend a great deal of their time frying fish. Neither does the task really need to be done — at least, there's only a very limited number of fish that need to be fried. Yet somehow, they all become so obsessed with resentment at the thought that some of their co-workers might be spending more time making cabinets, and not doing their fair share of the fish-frying responsibilities, that before long there's endless piles of useless badly cooked fish piling up all over the workshop and it's all that anyone really does.

I think this is actually a pretty accurate description of the moral dynamics of our own economy.

## What's necessary

Now, I realise any such argument is going to run into immediate objections: "who are you to say what jobs are really 'necessary'? What's necessary anyway? You're an anthropology professor, what's the 'need' for that?" (And indeed a lot of tabloid readers would take the existence of my job as the very definition of wasteful social expenditure.) And on one level, this is obviously true. There can be no objective measure of social value.

I would not presume to tell someone who is convinced they are making a meaningful contribution to the world that, really, they are not. But what about those people who are themselves convinced their jobs are meaningless?

Not long ago I got back in touch with a school friend who I hadn't seen since I was 12. I was amazed to discover that in the interim, he had become first a poet, then the front man in an indie rock band. I'd heard some of his songs on the radio having no idea the singer was someone I actually knew. He was obviously brilliant, innovative, and his work had unquestionably brightened and improved the lives of people all over the world. Yet, after a couple of unsuccessful albums, he'd lost his contract, and plagued with debts and a newborn daughter, ended up, as he put it, "taking the default choice of so many directionless folk: law school."

Now he's a corporate lawyer working in a prominent New York firm. He was the first to admit that his job was utterly meaningless, contributed nothing to the world, and, in his own estimation, should not really exist.

There's a lot of questions one could ask here, starting with, what does it say about our society that it seems to generate an extremely limited demand for talented poet-musicians, but an apparently infinite demand for specialists in corporate law? (Answer: if 1% of the population controls most of the disposable wealth, what we call "the market" reflects what they think is useful or important, not anybody else.)

But even more, it shows that most people in these jobs are ultimately aware of it. In fact, I'm not sure I've ever met a corporate lawyer who didn't think their job was bullshit.

The same goes for almost all the new industries outlined above. There is a whole class of salaried professionals that, should you meet them at parties and admit that you do something that might be considered interesting (an anthropologist, for example), will want to avoid even discussing their line of work entirely.

Give them a few drinks, and they will launch into tirades about how pointless and stupid their job really is.

This is a profound psychological violence here. How can one even begin to speak of dignity in labour when one secretly feels one's job should not exist? How can it not create a sense of deep rage and resentment.

Yet it is the peculiar genius of our society that its rulers have figured out a way, as in the case of the fish-fryers, to ensure that rage is directed precisely against those who actually do get to do meaningful work.

For instance: in our society, there seems a general rule that, the more obviously one's work benefits other people, the less one is likely to be paid for it. Again, an objective measure is hard to find, but one easy way to get a sense is to ask: what would happen were this entire class of people to simply disappear? Say what you like about nurses, garbage collectors, or mechanics, it's obvious that were they to vanish in a puff of smoke, the results would be immediate and catastrophic. A world without teachers or dock-workers would soon be in trouble, and even one without science fiction writers or ska musicians would clearly be a lesser place.

It's not entirely clear how humanity would suffer were all private equity CEOs, lobbyists, PR researchers, actuaries, telemarketers, bailiffs or legal consultants to similarly vanish. (Many suspect it might markedly improve.) Yet apart from a handful of well-touted exceptions (doctors), the rule holds surprisingly well.

Even more perverse, there seems to be a broad sense that this is the way things should be. This is one of the secret strengths of right-wing populism. You can see it when tabloids whip up resentment against tube workers for paralysing London during contract disputes: the very fact that tube workers can paralyse London shows that their work is actually necessary, but this seems to be precisely what annoys people.

It's even clearer in the US, where Republicans have had remarkable success mobilizing resentment against school teachers, or auto workers (and not, significantly, against the school administrators or auto industry managers who actually cause the problems) for their supposedly bloated wages and benefits.

It's as if they are being told "but you get to teach children! Or make cars! You get to have real jobs! And on top of that you have the nerve to also expect middle-class pensions and health care?"

If someone had designed a work regime perfectly suited to maintaining the power of finance capital, it's hard to see how they could have done a better job. Real, productive workers are relentlessly squeezed and exploited. The remainder are divided between a terrorised stratum of the — universally reviled — unemployed and a larger stratum who are basically paid to do nothing, in positions designed to make them identify with the perspectives and sensibilities of the ruling class (managers, administrators, etc) — and particularly its financial avatars — but, at the same time, foster a simmering resentment against anyone whose work has clear and undeniable social value.

Clearly, the system was never consciously designed. It emerged from almost a century of trial and error. But it is the only explanation for why, despite our technological capacities, we are not all working 3-4 hour days.

# WORK

by prole.info

*This extract from the prole.info collective's 2005 booklet WORK COMMUNITY POLITICS WAR offers "a graphical introduction to the world as we know it." Prole.info is a US-based radical website producing pamphlets and illustrated booklets explaining communist politics. The authors introduce their project, released on a Creative Commons licence, as follows:*

"Prole" is short for "proletarian" a word used by Karl Marx to describe the working class under capitalism. We are all the people in this society who do not own property or a business we can make money from, and therefore have to sell our time and energy to a boss--we are forced to work. Our work is the basis of this society.

We are not just a sociological category. Work, and the society that grows out of it are alienating and miserable for us. We are constantly fighting against the conditions of our lives. Simply standing up for our own interests brings us into conflict with bosses, bureaucrats, landlords, police and politicians everywhere. These everyday struggles are the starting point to undermining capitalism. We are not just the working class; we are the working class that struggles to do away with work and class, and the society built around them.

The experience of those who are forced to work, and who struggle against the society based on work, creates certain kinds of ideas. When we are actively fighting for our own interests, these ideas solidify into a subversive, anti-capitalist perspective. This has at times been called "communism" or "anarchism." We do not need political groups to bring us these ideas, but we do need to think about how to fight for ourselves.

...moving from natural disaster to terrorist attack... from new diet to new famine... from celebrity sex scandal to political corruption scandal... from religious war to economic miracle... from tantalizing new advertisement to clichés on tv complaining about the government... from suggestions on how to be the ideal lover to suggestions on how to keep sports fans from rioting... from new police shootings to new health problems...

The same processes are at work everywhere... in democratic and in totalitarian governments... in corporations and in mom n' pop businesses... in cheeseburgers and in tofu... in opera, in country music and in hip hop... in every country and in every language... in prisons, in schools, in hospitals, in factories, in office towers, in war zones and in grocery stores. Something is feeding off our lives and spitting back images of them in our faces.

That something is the product of our own activity–our everyday working lives sold hour after hour, week after week, generation after generation. We don't have property or a business we can make money from, so we are forced to sell our time and energy to someone else. We are the modern day working class—the proles.

# WORK

*"Capital is dead labour, that, vampire-like, only lives by sucking living labour, and lives the more, the more labour it sucks."*

Karl Marx

We don't work because we want to.
We work because we have no other way to make money.

We sell our time and energy to a boss in order to buy the things we need to survive.

We are brought together with other workers and assigned different tasks. We specialize in different aspects of the work and repeat these tasks over and over again.

Our time at work is not really part of our lives. It is dead time controlled by our bosses and managers.

During our time at work we make things that our bosses can sell. These things are objects like cotton shirts, computers and skyscrapers or qualities like clean floors and healthy patients or services like having a bus take you where you want to go, having a waiter take your order or having someone call you at home to try to get you to buy things you don't need.

The work is not done because of what it produces.
We do it to get paid, and the boss pays us for it to make a profit.

At the end of the day the bosses re-invest the money we make them, and enlarge their businesses. Our work is stored up in the things our bosses own and sell—capital.

They are always looking for new ways to store up our activity in things,

new markets to sell them to,

and new people with nothing to sell but their time and energy to work for them.

What we get from work is enough money to pay for rent, food, clothes and beer—enough to keep us coming back to work. When we're not at work, we spend time traveling to or from work, preparing for work, resting up because we're exhausted from work or getting drunk to forget about work.

The only thing worse than work, is not having it. Then we waste our weeks away looking for work, without getting paid for it. If welfare is available, it is a pain-in-the-ass to get and is never as much as working. The constant threat of unemployment is what keeps us going to work everyday.

And our work is the basis of this society. The power our bosses get from it expands every time we work. It is the dominant force in every country in the world.

At work we are under the control of our bosses, and of the markets they sell to. But an invisible hand imposes a work-like discipline and pointlessness on the rest of our lives as well. Life seems like a kind of show we watch from the outside, but have no control over.

All sorts of other activities tend to become as alienating, boring and stressful as work: housework, schoolwork, leisure. That's capitalism.

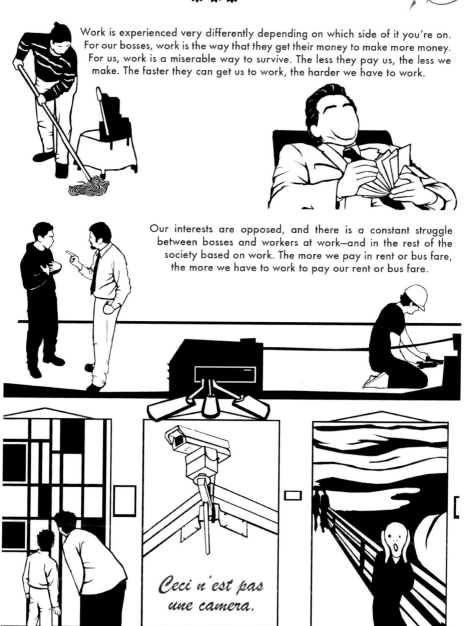

Work is experienced very differently depending on which side of it you're on. For our bosses, work is the way that they get their money to make more money. For us, work is a miserable way to survive. The less they pay us, the less we make. The faster they can get us to work, the harder we have to work.

Our interests are opposed, and there is a constant struggle between bosses and workers at work—and in the rest of the society based on work. The more we pay in rent or bus fare, the more we have to work to pay our rent or bus fare.

*Ceci n'est pas une camera.*

The current state of wages, benefits, hours and working conditions as well as politics, art and technology is a result of the current state of this class struggle. Simply standing up for our own interests in this struggle, is the starting point of undermining capitalism.

While these divisions and exclusive communities are being pushed on us from one side, an all-inclusive human community is sold to us from the other. This community is just as imaginary and false. It denies the basic division of society.

Business owners run the government and the media, the schools and prisons, the welfare offices and the police. We have our lives run by them.
The newspapers and television put forward their view of the world.
Schools teach about the great (or unfortunate) history of their society and produce a spectrum of graduates and dropouts fit for different kinds of work.
The government provides services to keep their society running smoothly.

And when all else fails, they have the police, the prisons and the army.

This is not our community.

They organize us against each other, but we can organize ourselves against them. The whole point of talking about class and "the proles" is to insist on the very basic way in which people from different "communities" have essentially similar experiences, and to show that people from the same "communities" should in fact hate each other. This is the starting point to fighting the existing communities. When we begin to fight for our own interests we see that others are doing the same thing. Prejudices fall away, and our anger is directed where it belongs.

We are not weak because we are divided. We are divided because we are weak.

The existing communities become irrelevant as they are attacked, and they are attacked by becoming irrelevant.

Racism and sexism are unappealing, when working men and women of different races are fighting their class enemies side by side. And that fight becomes more effective by involving people from different "communities".

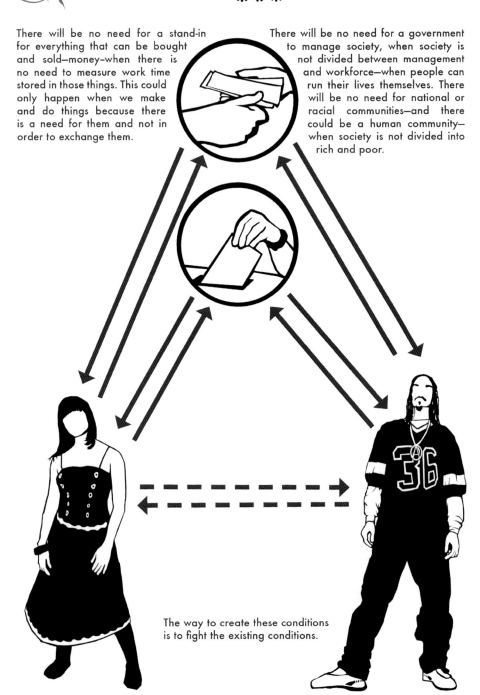

There will be no need for a stand-in for everything that can be bought and sold—money—when there is no need to measure work time stored in those things. This could only happen when we make and do things because there is a need for them and not in order to exchange them.

There will be no need for a government to manage society, when society is not divided between management and workforce—when people can run their lives themselves. There will be no need for national or racial communities—and there could be a human community—when society is not divided into rich and poor.

The way to create these conditions is to fight the existing conditions.

This tendency to create community by fighting against the conditions of our lives—and therefore against work, money, exchange, borders, nations, governments, police, religion, and race—has at times been called "communism".

When we start to fight against the conditions of our lives, a completely different kind of activity appears. We do not look for a politician to come change things for us. We do it ourselves, with other working class people. Whenever this kind of working class resistance breaks out, politicians try to extinguish it in a flood of petitions, lobbying and election campaigns. But when we are fighting for ourselves, our activity looks completely different from theirs. We take property away from landlords and use it for ourselves. We use militant tactics against our bosses and end up fighting with the police. We form groups where everyone takes part in the activity, and there is no division between leaders and followers. We do not fight for our leaders, for our bosses or for our country. We fight for ourselves.

This is not the ultimate form of democracy. We are imposing our needs on society without debate—needs that are directly contrary to the interests and wishes of rich people everywhere. There is no way for us to speak on equal terms with this society.

This tendency of working class struggles to go outside and against the government and politics, and to create new forms of organization that do not put our faith in anything other than our own ability, has at times been called "anarchism".

So we're in a war—a class war. There is no set of ideas, proposals and organizational strategies that can bring victory. There is no solution outside of winning the war.

So long as they have the initiative, we are separated, and passive. Our response to the conditions of our lives is individual: quitting our jobs, moving to neighborhoods with cheaper rent, joining subcultures and gangs, suicide, buying lottery tickets, drug abuse and alcoholism, going to church.

Their world looks like the only possibility. Any hope for change is lived on an imaginary level—separated from our everyday lives. It's business as usual, with all the crisis and destruction that this implies.

When we go on the offensive we begin to recognize each other and to fight collectively. We use the ways that society depends on us to disrupt it. We strike, sabotage, riot, desert, mutiny and take over property. We create organizations in order to amplify and coordinate our activities. All kinds of new possibilities open up.

We grow more daring and more aggressive in pursuing our own class interests. These do not lie in forming a new government, or becoming the new boss. Our interests lie in ending our own way of life—and therefore the society that is based on that way of life.

We are the working class who want to abolish work and class. We are the community of people who want to tear the existing community apart. Our political program is to destroy politics. In order to do that, we have to push the subversive tendencies that exist today until we have completely remade society everywhere. This has at times been called "revolution".

No working ideal for machine production can be based solely on the gospel of work; still less can it be based upon an uncritical belief in constantly raising the quantitative standard of consumption.

If we are to achieve a purposive and cultivated use of the enormous energies now happily at our disposal, we must examine in detail the processes that lead up to the final state of leisure, free activity, creation. It is because of the lapse and mismanagement of these processes that we have not reached the desirable end; and it is because of our failure to frame a comprehensive scheme of ends that we have not succeeded in achieving even the beginnings of social efficiency in the preparatory work.

LEWIS MUMFORD
Technics and Civilisation (1934)

# ALSO FROM FREEDOM...

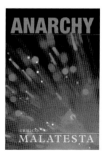

Anarchism without the syndicalism

**£5**

Anarchism in the everyday

**£7.50**

Red Action on the 1980s street war

**£15**

Loveable cartoon meets class struggle

**£8**

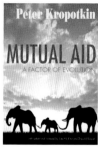

Famed rebuttal of social Darwinism

**£15**

Biography of the iconic 1910s rebel

**£9.50**

The surprising politics of Herbert Read

**£6**

A concise tale of anarcho-syndicalism

**£5**

Mental health guide for activists

**£4**

## DIRECT SALES AND ENQUIRIES

**Freedom Press**
Angel Alley,
84b Whitechapel High
Street, London
E1 7QX

**Telephone**
(07952) 157-742

**Email**
admin@
freedompress.org.uk

**Web**
freedompress.org.uk

**Social media**
@freedom_paper
facebook.com/
freedombookshop

**Trade orders may be placed via Central Books:**

50 Freshwater Road,
Chadwell Heath,
London RM8 1RX

Tel 44 (0)20 8525 8800
Fax 44 (0)20 8525 8879
contactus@central
books.com

centralbooks.com

# THIS SPACE HAS BEEN LEFT FREE, FOR IDLE DOODLING

Printed by print24
Typefaces: *Sunn* by Rit Creative, *Big John* by Ion Lucin and *Centabel Book*